Lord, what fools these mortals be!

A MIDSUMMER NIGHT'S DREAM
Act III, Scene 2

A Midsummer Night's Dream

with Connections

A Midsummer Night's Dream

William Shakespeare

with
Connections

HOLT, RINEHART AND WINSTON
Harcourt Brace & Company

Austin • New York • Orlando • Atlanta • San Francisco
Boston • Dallas • Toronto • London

For permission to reprint copyrighted material, grateful acknowledgment is made to the following sources:

Susan Bergholz Literary Services, New York: "Tin Tan Tan" from *Woman Hollering Creek* by Sandra Cisneros. Copyright © 1991 by Sandra Cisneros. Published by Vintage Books, a division of Random House, Inc., New York; originally published in hardcover by Random House, Inc. All rights reserved. **Richard Covington:** From "The Rebirth of Shakespeare's Globe" by Richard Covington from the *Smithsonian,* vol. 28, no. 8, November 1997. Copyright © 1997 by Richard Covington. **Alfred A. Knopf, a division of Random House, Inc.:** "The Laugher" from *The Stories of Heinrich Böll,* translated by Leila Vennewitz. Translation copyright © 1986 by Leila Vennewitz and the Estate of Heinrich Böll. **Leiber & Stoller Music:** Lyrics from "Love Potion Number Nine" by Jerry Leiber and Mike Stoller. Copyright © by Jerry Leiber and Mike Stoller. **Penguin Books Ltd.:** From "The Knight's Tale" from *The Canterbury Tales* by Geoffrey Chaucer, translated by Nevill Coghill (Penguin Classics 1951, fourth revised edition 1977). Copyright © 1951, 1958, 1960, 1975 and 1977 by Nevill Coghill. **Peters, Fraser & Dunlop Group Ltd.:** From "The Daily Round" from *How Shakespeare Spent the Day* by Ivor Brown. Copyright © 1963 by Ivor Brown. **Jay Walljasper:** From "Midsummer Night Is More than a Dream" by Jay Walljasper from *Utne Reader,* July/August. Copyright © 1993 by Jay Walljasper.

Cover: Joe Melomo, Design Director; ShoeHorn, Inc., Designer; Andrew Yates, Photographer; Betty Mayo, Photo Researcher

HRW is a registered trademark licensed to Holt, Rinehart and Winston.

Printed in the United States of America

ISBN 0-03-095765-6

6 7 8 9   043   07 06 05 04

Contents

CONTINUED

Dramatis Personae

THESEUS, Duke of Athens.
EGEUS, father to Hermia.
LYSANDER, DEMETRIUS, in love with Hermia.
PHILOSTRATE, Master of the Revels to Theseus.

QUINCE, a carpenter.
BOTTOM, a weaver.
FLUTE, a bellows-mender.
SNOUT, a tinker.
SNUG, a joiner.
STARVELING, a tailor
HIPPOLYTA, Queen of the Amazons, betrothed to Theseus.
HERMIA, daughter to Egeus, in love with Lysander
HELENA, in love with Demetrius.

OBERON, King of the Fairies.
TITANIA, Queen of the Fairies.
PUCK, or Robin Goodfellow.
PEASEBLOSSOM, COBWEB, MOTH, MUSTARDSEED, fairies.
Other FAIRIES attending their King and Queen; Attendants
on THESEUS and HIPPOLYTA

Act I

Scene 1. Athens. The palace of Theseus.

Enter THESEUS, HIPPOLYTA, PHILOSTRATE, *and*
ATTENDANTS.

Theseus.
> Now, fair Hippolyta, our nuptial hour
> Draws on apace. Four happy days bring in
> Another moon; but, O, methinks, how slow
> This old moon wanes! She lingers° my desires,
> Like a stepdame, or a dowager,   5
> Long withering out a young man's revenue.°

Hippolyta.
> Four days will quickly steep themselves in night;
> Four nights will quickly dream away the time;
> And then the moon, like to a silver bow
> New-bent in heaven, shall behold the night   10
> Of our solemnities.

Theseus.   Go, Philostrate,
> Stir up the Athenian youth to merriments,
> Awake the pert and nimble spirit of mirth,
> Turn melancholy forth to funerals;
> The pale companion° is not for our pomp.°   15

> > > > *Exit* PHILOSTRATE.

> Hippolyta, I wooed thee with my sword,°

I.1.4. **lingers:** delays the fulfillment of.
6.   **Long ... revenue:** slowly depleting the young man's money
    (presumably because he must support his widowed stepmother).
15.   **companion:** fellow. **pomp:** splendid ceremony.
16.   **I ... sword:** Theseus captured Hippolyta in a battle with the
    Amazons.

1

And won thy love, doing thee injuries;
But I will wed thee in another key,
With pomp, with triumph, and with reveling.

Enter EGEUS *and his daughter* HERMIA, LYSANDER,
and DEMETRIUS.

Egeus.
    Happy be Theseus, our renownèd duke!   20
Theseus.
    Thanks, good Egeus. What's the news
      with thee?
Egeus.
    Full of vexation come I, with complaint
    Against my child, my daughter Hermia.
    Stand forth, Demetrius. My noble lord,
    This man hath my consent to marry her.   25
    Stand forth, Lysander. And, my gracious duke,
    This man hath bewitched the bosom of my child.
    Thou, thou, Lysander, thou hast given her rhymes,
    And interchanged love tokens with my child.
    Thou hast by moonlight at her window sung,   30
    With feigning voice, verses of feigning love,
    And stol'n the impression of her fantasy°
    With bracelets of thy hair, rings, gauds, conceits,°
    Knacks, trifles, nosegays, sweetmeats, messengers
    Of strong prevailment in unhardened youth.   35
    With cunning hast thou filched my daughter's
      heart,
    Turned her obedience, which is due to me,
    To stubborn harshness. And, my gracious duke,
    Be it so she will not here before your grace
    Consent to marry with Demetrius,   40
    I beg the ancient privilege of Athens:
    As she is mine, I may dispose of her,
    Which shall be either to this gentleman

---

32.   **stol'n … fantasy:** dishonestly impressed her.
33.   **gauds, conceits:** trinkets, clever compliments.

Or to her death, according to our law
Immediately° provided in that case.   45
Theseus.
What say you, Hermia? Be advised, fair maid.
To you your father should be as a god,
One that composed your beauties; yea, and one
To whom you are but as a form in wax
By him imprinted and within his power   50
To leave the figure or disfigure it.
Demetrius is a worthy gentleman.
Hermia.
So is Lysander.
Theseus.   In himself he is;
But in this kind, wanting your father's voice,°
The other must be held the worthier.   55
Hermia.
I would my father looked but with my eyes.
Theseus.
Rather your eyes must with his judgment look.
Hermia.
I do entreat your grace to pardon me.
I know not by what power I am made bold,
Nor how it may concern my modesty,   60
In such a presence here to plead my thoughts;
But I beseech your grace that I may know
The worst that may befall me in this case,
If I refuse to wed Demetrius
Theseus.
Either to die the death, or to abjure   65
Forever the society of men.
Therefore, fair Hermia, question your desires;
Know of° your youth, examine well your blood,°
Whether, if you yield not to your father's choice,

---

45.   **Immediately:** directly, expressly.
54.   **But ... voice:** but in this respect (as a husband), lacking your
           father's consent.
68.   **Know of:** consider. **blood:** emotions, passions.

You can endure the livery of a nun,   70
For aye to be in shady cloister mewed,°
To live a barren sister all your life,
Chanting faint hymns to the cold fruitless moon.°
Thrice-blessèd they that master so their blood,
To undergo such maiden pilgrimage;   75
But earthlier happy is the rose distilled,°
Than that which, withering on the virgin thorn,
Grows, lives, and dies in single blessedness.

Hermia.

So will I grow, so live, so die, my lord,
Ere I will yield my virgin patent° up   80
Unto his lordship, whose unwished yoke
My soul consents not to give sovereignty.

Theseus.

Take time to pause; and, by the next new moon—
The sealing day betwixt my love and me,
For everlasting bond of fellowship—   85
Upon that day either prepare to die
For disobedience to your father's will,
Or else to wed Demetrius, as he would,
Or on Diana's altar to protest
For aye austerity and single life.   90

Demetrius.

Relent, sweet Hermia: and, Lysander, yield
Thy crazèd title° to my certain right.

Lysander.

You have her father's love, Demetrius;
Let me have Hermia's: do you marry him.

Egeus.

Scornful Lysander! True, he hath my love,   95

---

71.   **mewed:** caged, imprisoned.
73.   **moon:** Diana, goddess of chastity.
76.   **distilled:** made into perfume (rather than left pure and
     untouched).
80.   **virgin patent:** privilege of virginity.
92.   **crazèd title:** unsound claim.

And what is mine my love shall render him.
And she is mine, and all my right of her
I do estate unto° Demetrius.

Lysander.

I am, my lord, as well derived as he,
As well possessed;° my love is more than his;   100
My fortunes every way as fairly ranked
(If not with vantage) as Demetrius';
And, which is more than all these boasts can be,
I am beloved of beauteous Hermia.
Why should not I then prosecute my right?   105
Demetrius, I'll avouch it to his head,
Made love to Nedar's daughter, Helena,
And won her soul; and she, sweet lady, dotes,
Devoutly dotes, dotes in idolatry,
Upon this spotted° and inconstant man.   110

Theseus.

I must confess that I have heard so much,
And with Demetrius thought to have spoke
     thereof;
But, being overfull of self-affairs,
My mind did lose it. But, Demetrius, come;
And come, Egeus. You shall go with me;   115
I have some private schooling for you both.
For you, fair Hermia, look you arm yourself
To fit your fancies to your father's will;
Or else the law of Athens yields you up—
Which by no means we may extenuate—   120
To death, or to a vow of single life.
Come, my Hippolyta. What cheer, my love?
Demetrius and Egeus, go along.
I must employ you in some business
Against° our nuptial, and confer with you   125

---

98. **estate unto:** bestow upon.
100. **As well possessed:** as wealthy.
110. **spotted:** morally stained, untrustworthy.
125. **Against:** in preparation for.

Of something nearly that° concerns yourselves.

Egeus.

With duty and desire we follow you.

Exeunt all but LYSANDER *and* HERMIA.

Lysander.

How now, my love! Why is your cheek so pale?
How chance° the roses there do fade so fast?

Hermia.

Belike° for want of rain, which I could well   130
Beteem° them from the tempest of my eyes.

Lysander.

Ay me! For aught that I could ever read,
Could ever hear by tale or history,
The course of true love never did run smooth;
But, either it was different in blood—   135

Hermia.

O cross! Too high to be enthralled to low!

Lysander.

Or else misgraffèd° in respect of years—

Hermia.

O spite! Too old to be engaged to young!

Lysander.

Or else it stood upon the choice of friends—

Hermia.

O hell! To choose love by another's eyes!   140

Lysander.

Or, if there were a sympathy in choice,
War, death, or sickness did lay siege to it,
Making it momentany° as a sound,
Swift as a shadow, short as any dream,

---

126. **nearly that:** that closely.
129. **How chance:** how does it come about that.
130. **Belike:** maybe, very likely.
131. **Beteem:** grant, bestow upon.
137. **misgraffèd:** ill suited, poorly matched.
143. **momentany:** momentary, passing quickly.

Brief as the lightning in the collied° night,   145
That, in a spleen,° unfolds both heaven and earth,
And ere a man hath power to say, "Behold!"
The jaws of darkness do devour it up:
So quick bright things come to confusion.

Hermia.

If then true lovers have been ever crossed,   150
It stands as an edict in destiny:
Then let us teach our trial patience,°
Because it is a customary cross,
As due to love as thoughts and dreams and sighs,
Wishes and tears, poor Fancy's° followers.   155

Lysander.

A good persuasion.° Therefore, hear me, Hermia.
I have a widow aunt, a dowager
Of great revenue, and she hath no child.
From Athens is her house remote seven leagues,
And she respects me as her only son.   160
There, gentle Hermia, may I marry thee,
And to that place the sharp Athenian law
Cannot pursue us. If thou lovest me, then,
Steal forth thy father's house tomorrow night;
And in the wood, a league without the town,   165
Where I did meet thee once with Helena,
To do observance to a morn of May,
There will I stay for thee.

Hermia   My good Lysander!
I swear to thee, by Cupid's strongest bow,
By his best arrow with the golden head,°   170
By the simplicity of Venus' doves,
By that which knitteth souls and prospers loves,

---

145. **collied:** darkened, murky.
146. **spleen:** flash or fit of passion.
152. **teach ... patience:** teach ourselves to be patient during this trial.
155. **Fancy's:** love's.
156. **persuasion:** principle, conviction.
170. **arrow ... head:** Cupid's golden-headed arrows caused love; the leaden-headed ones caused contempt.

And by that fire which burned the Carthage queen,°
When the false Troyan under sail was seen,
By all the vows that ever men have broke,   175
In number more than ever women spoke,
In that same place thou hast appointed me,
Tomorrow truly will I meet with thee.

Lysander.
Keep promise, love. Look, here comes Helena.

Enter HELENA.

Hermia.
God speed fair Helena! Whither away?   180
Helena.
Call you me fair? That fair again unsay.
Demetrius loves your fair.° O happy fair!
Your eyes are lodestars,° and your tongue's sweet
      air°
More tunable than lark to shepherd's ear,
When wheat is green, when hawthorn buds
      appear.   185
Sickness is catching. O, were favor° so,
Yours would I catch, fair Hermia, ere I go;
My ear should catch your voice, my eye your eye,
My tongue should catch your tongue's sweet
      melody.
Were the world mine, Demetrius being bated,°   190
The rest I'd give to be to you translated.°
O, teach me how you look, and with what art
You sway the motion of Demetrius' heart!
Hermia.
I frown upon him, yet he loves me still.

---

173. **Carthage queen:** Dido (who threw herself on a funeral pyre
         when her lover, the Trojan Aeneas, left her).
182. **your fair:** your type of beauty (probably blond).
183. **lodestars:** guiding stars. **air:** music.
186. **favor:** good looks.
190. **bated:** not included, excepted.
191. **translated:** transformed.

Helena.

O that your frowns would teach my smiles
    such skill! 195

Hermia.

I give him curses, yet he gives me love.

Helena.

O that my prayers could such affection move!

Hermia.

The more I hate, the more he follows me.

Helena.

The more I love, the more he hateth me.

Hermia.

His folly, Helena, is no fault of mine. 200

Helena.

None, but your beauty: would that fault were mine!

Hermia.

Take comfort. He no more shall see my face;
Lysander and myself will fly this place.
Before the time I did Lysander see,
Seemed Athens as a paradise to me. 205
O, then, what graces in my love do dwell,
That he hath turned a heaven unto a hell!

Lysander.

Helen, to you our minds we will unfold.
Tomorrow night, when Phoebe° doth behold
Her silver visage in the wat'ry glass, 210
Decking with liquid pearl the bladed grass,
A time that lovers' flights doth still° conceal,
Through Athens' gates have we devised to steal.

Hermia.

And in the wood, where often you and I
Upon faint primrose beds were wont to lie, 215
Emptying our bosoms of their counsel sweet,
There my Lysander and myself shall meet,
And thence from Athens turn away our eyes,

---

209. **Phoebe:** the moon, or Diana.
212. **still:** always.

To seek new friends and stranger companies.
Farewell, sweet playfellow. Pray thou for us;　　220
And good luck grant thee thy Demetrius!
Keep word, Lysander. We must starve our sight
From lovers' food till tomorrow deep midnight.

Lysander.
I will, my Hermia. [*Exit* HERMIA.] Helena, adieu.
As you on him, Demetrius dote on you!　　225

　　　　　　　　　　Exit LYSANDER.

Helena.
How happy some o'er other some° can be!
Through Athens I am thought as fair as she.
But what of that? Demetrius thinks not so;
He will not know what all but he do know.
And as he errs, doting on Hermia's eyes,　　230
So I, admiring of his qualities.
Things base and vile, holding no quantity,°
Love can transpose to form and dignity.
Love looks not with the eyes, but with the mind,
And therefore is winged Cupid painted blind.　　235
Nor hath Love's mind of any judgment taste;
Wings, and no eyes, figure° unheedy haste:
And therefore is Love said to be a child,
Because in choice he is so oft beguiled.
As waggish boys in game themselves forswear,　　240
So the boy Love is perjured everywhere.
For ere Demetrius looked on Hermia's eyne,°
He hailed down oaths that he was only mine;
And when this hail some heat from Hermia felt,
So he dissolved, and show'rs of oaths did melt.　　245
I will go tell him of fair Hermia's flight.
Then to the wood will he tomorrow night

---

226. some ... some: some compared with others.
232. holding no quantity: unshapely, ungainly, having no proportion.
237. figure: are a symbol of.
242. eyne: eyes.

Pursue her; and for this intelligence
If I have thanks, it is a dear expense:°
But herein mean I to enrich my pain,   250
To have his sight thither and back again.

Exit.

Scene 2. *Athens. Quince's house.*

Enter QUINCE, SNUG, BOTTOM, FLUTE, SNOUT, *and*
STARVELING.

Quince. Is all our company here?
Bottom. You were best to call them generally,° man
    by man, according to the scrip.
Quince. Here is the scroll of every man's name, which
    is thought fit, through all Athens, to play in our   5
    interlude before the duke and the duchess, on his
    wedding day at night.
Bottom. First, good Peter Quince, say what the play
    treats on; then read the names of the actors; and
    so grow to a point.   10
Quince. Marry,° our play is, "The most lamentable
    comedy, and most cruel death of Pyramus and
    Thisby."
Bottom. A very good piece of work, I assure you, and a
    merry. Now, good Peter Quince, call forth your   15
    actors by the scroll. Masters, spread yourselves.
Quince. Answer as I call you. Nick Bottom, the weaver.
Bottom. Ready. Name what part I am for, and proceed.
Quince. You, Nick Bottom, are set down for Pyramus.
Bottom. What is Pyramus? A lover, or a tyrant?   20
Quince. A lover that kills himself, most gallant,
    for love.
Bottom. That will ask some tears in the true

---

249.   **dear expense:** expense gladly undertaken.
I.2.2. **generally:** an example of Bottom's misuse of words; he means
    individually.
11.   **Marry:** a mild oath, originally "by the Virgin Mary."

performing of it: if I do it, let the audience look to
their eyes. I will move storms, I will condole° in   25
some measure. To the rest: yet my chief humor°
is for a tyrant. I could play Ercles° rarely, or a part
to tear a cat in,° to make all split.

> The raging rocks
> And shivering shocks   30
> Shall break the locks
>   Of prison gates;
> And Phibbus' car°
> Shall shine from far,
> And make and mar   35
>   The foolish Fates.

This was lofty! Now name the rest of the players.
This is Ercles' vein, a tyrant's vein. A lover is
more condoling.
Quince. Francis Flute, the bellows mender.   40
Flute. Here, Peter Quince.
Quince. Flute, you must take Thisby on you.
Flute. What is Thisby? A wand'ring knight?
Quince. It is the lady that Pyramus must love.
Flute. Nay, faith, let not me play a woman. I have   45
a beard coming.
Quince. That's all one.° You shall play it in a mask,
and you may speak as small° as you will.
Bottom. An° I may hide my face, let me play Thisby

---

25. **condole:** act mournful, lament.
26. **humor:** inclination, preference.
27. **Ercles:** Hercules (a part noted for its ranting).
27–28. **part ... in:** part that calls for much ranting and railing.
33. **Phibbus' car:** mispronunciation of *Phoebus' car*, or chariot,
     meaning the sun.
47. **That's all one:** It doesn't matter.
48. **small:** softly, thinly.
49. **An:** if.

too. I'll speak in a monstrous little voice, "Thisne,° 50
Thisne!" "Ah Pyramus, my lover dear! Thy Thisby
dear, and lady dear!"

Quince. No, no; you must play Pyramus: and, Flute,
you Thisby.

Bottom. Well, proceed. 55

Quince. Robin Starveling, the tailor.

Starveling. Here, Peter Quince.

Quince. Robin Starveling, you must play Thisby's
mother. Tom Snout, the tinker.

Snout. Here, Peter Quince. 60

Quince. You, Pyramus' father: myself, Thisby's
father: Snug, the joiner; you, the lion's part. And
I hope here is a play fitted.

Snug. Have you the lion's part written? Pray you, if
it be, give it me, for I am slow to study. 65

Quince. You may do it extempore, for it is nothing
but roaring.

Bottom. Let me play the lion too. I will roar that I
will do any man's heart good to hear me. I will
roar, that I will make the duke say, "Let him roar 70
again, let him roar again."

Quince. An you should do it too terribly, you would
fright the duchess and the ladies, that they would
shriek; and that were enough to hang us all.

All. That would hang us, every mother's son. 75

Bottom. I grant you, friends, if you should fright the
ladies out of their wits, they would have no more
discretion but to hang us: but I will aggravate° my
voice so that I will roar you as gently as any
sucking dove; I will roar you an 'twere° any 80
nightingale.

Quince. You can play no part but Pyramus; for Pyramus

---

50. **Thisne:** Perhaps Shakespeare was punning on the similarity of
this word, meaning "in this manner," to *Thisby*.
78. **aggravate:** Bottom means *moderate*.
80. **an 'twere:** as if it were.

is a sweet-faced man; a proper° man as one shall
see in a summer's day; a most lovely, gentleman-
like man: therefore you must needs play Pyramus. 85
Bottom. Well, I will undertake it. What beard were
I best to play it in?
Quince. Why, what you will.
Bottom. I will discharge it in either your straw-color
beard, your orange-tawny beard, your purple-in- 90
grain° beard, or your French-crown-color° beard,
your perfit° yellow.
Quince. Some of your French crowns° have no hair
at all, and then you will play barefaced. But,
masters, here are your parts; and I am to entreat 95
you, request you, and desire you, to con° them by
tomorrow night; and meet me in the palace wood,
a mile without the town, by moonlight. There will
we rehearse, for if we meet in the city, we shall be
dogged with company, and our devices° known. 100
In the meantime I will draw a bill of properties,
such as our play wants. I pray you, fail me not.
Bottom. We will meet; and there we may rehearse
most obscenely° and courageously. Take pains; be
perfit: adieu. 105
Quince. At the Duke's Oak we meet.
Bottom. Enough; hold or cut bowstrings.

Exeunt.

---

83. **proper:** handsome.
90–91. **purple-in-grain:** dyed with a deep purple.
91. **French-crown-color:** color of a French gold coin.
92. **perfit:** perfect.
93. **crowns:** punning on two meanings: gold crowns and the crowns of
     heads gone bald from the so-called French disease (syphilis).
96. **con:** study, learn by heart.
100. **devices:** plans.
104. **obscenely:** Bottom means *seemly.*

Act II

Scene 1. A wood near Athens.

Enter, from opposite sides, a FAIRY *and* PUCK.

Puck.
How now, spirit! Whither wander you?
Fairy.
    Over hill, over dale,
      Thorough bush, thorough brier,
    Over park, over pale,°
      Thorough flood, thorough fire,   5
    I do wander everywhere,
    Swifter than the moon's sphere;°
    And I serve the Fairy Queen,
    To dew her orbs° upon the green.
    The cowslips tall her pensioners° be: 10
    In their gold coats spots you see;
    Those be rubies, fairy favors,
    In those freckles live their savors.°
I must go seek some dewdrops here,
And hang a pearl in every cowslip's ear.   15
Farewell, thou lob° of spirits; I'll be gone.
Our queen and all her elves come here anon.

II.1.4. **pale:** enclosed field, park.
7. **moon's sphere:** In Shakespeare's day, the moon was believed to be fixed in a hollow sphere that moved around the earth.
9. **orbs:** fairy rings (circles of dark grass).
10. **pensioners:** bodyguards, here referring to Elizabeth I's guard of fifty handsome young noblemen.
13. **savors:** perfumes.
16. **lob:** clod, clumsy fellow.

Puck.
> The king doth keep his revels here tonight.
> Take heed the queen come not within his sight.
> For Oberon is passing fell and wrath,°   20
> Because that she as her attendant hath
> A lovely boy, stolen from an Indian king;
> She never had so sweet a changeling.°
> And jealous Oberon would have the child
> Knight of his train, to trace° the forests wild.   25
> But she perforce withholds the lovèd boy,
> Crowns him with flowers, and makes him all
>   her joy.
> And now they never meet in grove or green,
> By fountain clear, or spangled starlight sheen,
> But they do square,° that all their elves for fear   30
> Creep into acorn cups and hide them there.

Fairy.
> Either I mistake your shape and making quite,
> Or else you are that shrewd and knavish sprite
> Called Robin Goodfellow. Are not you he
> That frights the maidens of the villagery,   35
> Skim milk, and sometimes labor in the quern,°
> And bootless° make the breathless housewife churn,
> And sometime make the drink to bear no barm,°
> Mislead night wanderers, laughing at their harm?
> Those that Hobgoblin call you, and sweet Puck,   40
> You do their work, and they shall have good luck.
> Are not you he?

---

20. **passing … wrath:** full of anger.
23. **changeling:** usually refers to a fairy child that fairies exchange
     for a human child they have stolen. Here, it is applied to the
     stolen human child.
25. **trace:** travel, traverse.
30. **square:** quarrel.
36. **quern:** hand mill for grinding grain.
37. **bootless:** vainly, uselessly.
38. **barm:** yeast, froth on ale.

Puck.   Thou speakest aright;
I am that merry wanderer of the night.
I jest to Oberon, and make him smile,
When I a fat and bean-fed horse beguile,   45
Neighing in likeness of a filly foal:
And sometime lurk I in a gossip's° bowl,
In very likeness of a roasted crab;°
And when she drinks, against her lips I bob
And on her withered dewlap° pour the ale.   50
The wisest aunt, telling the saddest tale,
Sometime for three-foot stool mistaketh me;
Then slip I from her bum, down topples she,
And "tailor"° cries, and falls into a cough;
And then the whole quire° hold their hips and
     laugh,   55
And waxen° in their mirth, and neeze,° and swear
A merrier hour was never wasted° there.
But, room, fairy! Here comes Oberon.
Fairy.
And here my mistress. Would that he were gone!

Enter, from one side, OBERON *with his train; from
the other,* TITANIA *with hers.*

Oberon.
Ill met by moonlight, proud Titania.   60
Titania.
What, jealous Oberon! Fairy, skip hence.
I have forsworn his bed and company.

---

47. **gossip's:** old woman's.
48. **crab:** crab apple.
50. **dewlap:** loose fold of skin around the neck.
54. **tailor:** perhaps suggesting the customary position of a tailor
     in Shakespeare's time, sitting on the ground.
55. **quire:** group, choir.
56. **waxen:** increase. **neeze:** sneeze.
57. **wasted:** passed.

Oberon.
   Tarry, rash wanton;° am not I thy lord?
Titania.
   Then I must be thy lady: but I know
   When thou hast stolen away from fairy land   65
   And in the shape of Corin° sat all day,
   Playing on pipes of corn, and versing love
   To amorous Phillida. Why art thou here,
   Come from the farthest steep of India?
   But that, forsooth, the bouncing° Amazon,   70
   Your buskined° mistress and your warrior love,
   To Theseus must be wedded, and you come
   To give their bed joy and prosperity.
Oberon.
   How canst thou thus for shame, Titania,
   Glance at my credit with Hippolyta,   75
   Knowing I know thy love to Theseus?
   Didst not thou lead him through the glimmering
      night
   From Perigenia, whom he ravishèd?
   And make him with fair Aegles break his faith,
   With Ariadne and Antiopa?°   80
Titania.
   These are the forgeries of jealousy:
   And never, since the middle summer's spring,°
   Met we on hill, in dale, forest, or mead,
   By pavèd fountain or by rushy brook,
   Or in the beachèd margent° of the sea,   85
   To dance our ringlets to the whistling wind,
   But with thy brawls thou hast disturbed our sport.

---

63.   **rash wanton:** hasty, headstrong creature.
66.   **Corin:** a conventional name for a lover in pastoral poetry.
70.   **bouncing:** swaggering.
71.   **buskined:** wearing hunter's boots (buskins).
78–80. **Perigenia ... Antiopa:** women Theseus loved and then abandoned.
82.   **middle summer's spring:** beginning of midsummer.
85.   **margent:** margin, shore.

Therefore the winds, piping to us in vain,
As in revenge, have sucked up from the sea
Contagious fogs; which, falling in the land,   90
Hath every pelting° river made so proud,
That they have overborne their continents.°
The ox hath therefore stretched his yoke in vain,
The plowman lost his sweat, and the green corn
Hath rotted ere his youth attained a beard;   95
The fold stands empty in the drownèd field,
And crows are fatted with the murrion flock;°
The nine men's morris° is filled up with mud;
And the quaint mazes° in the wanton green,°
For lack of tread, are undistinguishable.   100
The human mortals want their winter here;
No night is now with hymn or carol blest.
Therefore the moon, the governess of floods,
Pale in her anger, washes all the air,
That rheumatic diseases do abound.   105
And thorough this distemperature° we see
The seasons alter: hoary-headed frosts
Fall in the fresh lap of the crimson rose,
And on old Hiems'° thin and icy crown
An odorous chaplet° of sweet summer buds   110
Is, as in mockery, set. The spring, the summer,
The childing° autumn, angry winter, change
Their wonted liveries;° and the mazèd° world,

---

91. **pelting:** petty.
92. **continents:** confines, banks.
97. **murrion flock:** cattle or sheep killed by a disease called murrain.
98. **nine men's morris:** squares for a game played on the ground, with
     each player having nine "men."
99. **quaint mazes:** intricate paths through the grass. **wanton green:**
     grass growing wild.
106. **distemperature:** disorder in nature.
109. **old Hiems':** winter's.
110. **chaplet:** wreath, garland.
112. **childing:** fruitful, abundant.
113. **wonted liveries:** usual clothing. **mazèd:** amazed, bewildered.

By their increase, now knows not which is which.
And this same progeny of evils comes   115
From our debate, from our dissension;
We are their parents and original.

Oberon.
Do you amend it, then; it lies in you:
Why should Titania cross her Oberon?
I do but beg a little changeling boy,   120
To be my henchman.°

Titania.   Set your heart at rest.
The fairy land buys not° the child of me.
His mother was a vot'ress° of my order,
And, in the spicèd Indian air, by night,
Full often hath she gossiped by my side,   125
And sat with me on Neptune's yellow sands,
Marking th' embarkèd traders on the flood;
When we have laughed to see the sails conceive
And grow big-bellied with the wanton wind;
Which she, with pretty and with swimming gait   130
Following—her womb then rich with my young
     squire—
Would imitate, and sail upon the land,
To fetch me trifles, and return again,
As from a voyage, rich with merchandise.
But she, being mortal, of that boy did die;   135
And for her sake do I rear up her boy,
And for her sake I will not part with him.

Oberon.
How long within this wood intend you stay?

Titania.
Perchance till after Theseus' wedding day.
If you will patiently dance in our round,°   140

---

121. **henchman:** personal servant, page.
122. **The ... not:** not even the whole of your fairy kingdom could buy.
123. **vot'ress:** woman who has taken a vow.
140. **round:** dance done in a circle.

And see our moonlight revels, go with us.
If not, shun me, and I will spare° your haunts.

Oberon.

Give me that boy, and I will go with thee.

Titania.

Not for thy fairy kingdom. Fairies, away!
We shall chide downright, if I longer stay.   145

Exit TITANIA *with her train.*

Oberon.

Well, go thy way. Thou shalt not from this grove
Till I torment thee for this injury.
My gentle Puck, come hither. Thou rememb'rest
Since once I sat upon a promontory,
And heard a mermaid, on a dolphin's back,   150
Uttering such dulcet and harmonious breath,
That the rude sea grew civil at her song,
And certain stars shot madly from their spheres,
To hear the sea maid's music.

Puck.   I remember.

Oberon.

That very time I saw, but thou couldst not,   155
Flying between the cold moon and the earth,
Cupid all armed. A certain aim he took
At a fair vestal° thronèd by the west,
And loosed his love shaft smartly from his bow,
As it should° pierce a hundred thousand hearts.   160
But I might° see young Cupid's fiery shaft
Quenched in the chaste beams of the wat'ry moon,
And the imperial vot'ress passèd on,
In maiden meditation, fancy-free.°
Yet marked I where the bolt of Cupid fell.   165

---

142. **spare:** avoid, keep away from.
158. **vestal:** virgin (possibly a reference to Elizabeth I).
160. **As it should:** as if it should.
161. **might:** could.
164. **fancy-free:** not under the spell of love.

It fell upon a little western flower,
Before milk-white, now purple with love's wound,
And maidens call it love-in-idleness.°
Fetch me that flow'r; the herb I showed thee
    once:
The juice of it on sleeping eyelids laid   170
Will make or man or woman madly dote
Upon the next live creature that it sees.
Fetch me this herb, and be thou here again
Ere the leviathan° can swim a league.

Puck.
I'll put a girdle round about the earth   175
In forty minutes.

                                  Exit.

Oberon.   Having once this juice,
I'll watch Titania when she is asleep,
And drop the liquor of it in her eyes.
The next thing then she waking looks upon,
Be it on lion, bear, or wolf, or bull,   180
On meddling monkey, or on busy° ape,
She shall pursue it with the soul of love.
And ere I take this charm from off her sight,
As I can take it with another herb,
I'll make her render up her page to me.   185
But who comes here? I am invisible,
And I will overhear their conference.

Enter DEMETRIUS, HELENA *following him.*

Demetrius.
I love thee not, therefore pursue me not.
Where is Lysander and fair Hermia?
The one I'll slay, the other slayeth me.   190
Thou told'st me they were stol'n unto this wood;

---

168. **love-in-idleness:** pansy.
174. **leviathan:** whale, huge sea creature.
181. **busy:** interfering, meddlesome.

And here am I, and wood° within this wood,
Because I cannot meet my Hermia.
Hence, get thee gone, and follow me no more!
Helena.
    You draw me, you hardhearted adamant;°   195
But yet you draw not iron, for my heart
Is true as steel. Leave you your power to draw,
And I shall have no power to follow you.
Demetrius.
    Do I entice you? Do I speak you fair?°
Or, rather, do I not in plainest truth   200
Tell you, I do not nor I cannot love you?
Helena.
    And even for that do I love you the more.
I am your spaniel; and, Demetrius,
The more you beat me, I will fawn on you.
Use me but as your spaniel, spurn me, strike me,   205
Neglect me, lose me; only give me leave,
Unworthy as I am, to follow you.
What worser place can I beg in your love—
And yet a place of high respect with me—
Than to be usèd as you use your dog?   210
Demetrius.
    Tempt not too much the hatred of my spirit,
For I am sick when I do look on thee.
Helena.
    And I am sick when I look not on you.
Demetrius.
    You do impeach° your modesty too much,
To leave the city, and commit yourself   215
Into the hands of one that loves you not,
To trust the opportunity of night

---

192. **wood:** out of my mind (a pun on *wood* and possibly on *wooed*).
195. **adamant:** very hard gem, lodestone, magnet.
199. **speak you fair:** speak to you gently.
214. **impeach:** open to question.

And the ill counsel of a desert° place
With the rich worth of your virginity.

Helena.

Your virtue is my privilege.° For that   220
It is not night when I do see your face,
Therefore I think I am not in the night;
Nor doth this wood lack worlds of company,
For you in my respect° are all the world.
Then how can it be said I am alone,   225
When all the world is here to look on me?

Demetrius.

I'll run from thee and hide me in the brakes,°
And leave thee to the mercy of wild beasts.

Helena.

The wildest hath not such a heart as you.
Run when you will, the story shall be changed: 230
Apollo flies, and Daphne° holds the chase;
The dove pursues the griffin;° the mild hind°
Makes speed to catch the tiger; bootless speed,
When cowardice pursues, and valor flies.

Demetrius.

I will not stay° thy questions. Let me go!   235
O, if thou follow me, do not believe
But I shall do thee mischief in the wood.

Helena.

Ay, in the temple, in the town, the field,
You do me mischief. Fie, Demetrius!
Your wrongs do set a scandal on my sex.   240
We cannot fight for love, as men may do;

---

218. **desert:** deserted, wild.
220. **Your ... privilege:** your goodness is my guarantee.
224. **in my respect:** in my opinion.
227. **brakes:** bushes, thicket.
231. **Daphne:** a nymph who fled from Apollo and was changed into a laurel tree at her own request.
232. **griffin:** mythical monster with the head of an eagle and the body of a lion. **hind:** female deer.
235. **stay:** wait for.

We should be wooed, and were not made to woo.

Exit DEMETRIUS.

I'll follow thee, and make a heaven of hell,
To die upon° the hand I love so well.

Exit.

Oberon.
Fare thee well, nymph: ere he do leave this
   grove,   245
Thou shalt fly him, and he shall seek thy love.

Enter PUCK.

Hast thou the flower there? Welcome, wanderer.
Puck.
Ay, there it is.
Oberon.   I pray thee, give it me.
I know a bank where the wild thyme blows,
Where oxlips and the nodding violet grows,   250
Quite overcanopied with luscious woodbine,
With sweet musk roses, and with eglantine.
There sleeps Titania sometime of the night,
Lulled in these flowers with dances and delight;
And there the snake throws° her enameled skin,   255
Weed° wide enough to wrap a fairy in.
And with the juice of this I'll streak her eyes,
And make her full of hateful fantasies.
Take thou some of it, and seek through this grove.
A sweet Athenian lady is in love   260
With a disdainful youth. Anoint his eyes;
But do it when the next thing he espies
May be the lady. Thou shalt know the man
By the Athenian garments he hath on.
Effect it with some care that he may prove   265

---

244. **To die upon:** dying by.
255. **throws:** sheds, casts off.
256. **Weed:** wrap, garment.

More fond on her° than she upon her love:
And look thou meet me ere the first cock crow.
Puck.
Fear not, my lord, your servant shall do so.

Exeunt.

Scene 2. Another part of the wood.

Enter TITANIA *with her train.*

Titania.
Come, now a roundel° and a fairy song;
Then, for the third part of a minute, hence;
Some to kill cankers in the musk-rose buds,
Some war with reremice° for their leathern wings
To make my small elves coats, and some keep back   5
The clamorous owl, that nightly hoots and wonders
At our quaint° spirits. Sing me now asleep.
Then to your offices, and let me rest.

The FAIRIES *sing.*

First Fairy.
You spotted snakes with double tongue,
    Thorny hedgehogs, be not seen;   10
Newts and blindworms,° do no wrong,
    Come not near our Fairy Queen.
Chorus.
    Philomele,° with melody
    Sing in our sweet lullaby;

---

266. **fond on her:** foolishly doting on her.
II.2.1. roundel: dance done in a circle.
4.   **reremice:** bats.
7.   **quaint:** dainty.
11.   **blindworms:** small snakes.
13.   **Philomele:** nightingale.

Lulla, lulla, lullaby, lulla, lulla, lullaby: 15
　　Never harm
　　Nor spell nor charm,
Come our lovely lady nigh;
So, good night, with lullaby.

First Fairy.

Weaving spiders, come not here;   20
　　Hence, you long-legged spinners, hence!
Beetles black, approach not near;
　　Worm nor snail, do no offense.

Chorus.

Philomele, with melody, &c.

Second Fairy.

Hence, away! Now all is well.   25
One aloof stand sentinel.

Exeunt FAIRIES. TITANIA *sleeps.*

Enter OBERON *and squeezes the flower on* TITANIA'*s eyelids.*

Oberon.

What thou see'st when thou dost wake,
Do it for thy truelove take;
Love and languish for his sake.
Be it ounce,° or cat, or bear,   30
Pard,° or boar with bristled hair,
In thy eye that shall appear
When thou wak'st, it is thy dear.
Wake when some vile thing is near.

Exit.

Enter LYSANDER *and* HERMIA.

Lysander.

Fair love, you faint with wand'ring in the wood;   35

30.　**ounce:** lynx.
31.　**Pard:** leopard.

And to speak troth,° I have forgot our way.
We'll rest us, Hermia, if you think it good,
And tarry for the comfort of the day.
Hermia.
Be't so, Lysander. Find you out a bed;
For I upon this bank will rest my head.   40
Lysander.
One turf shall serve as pillow for us both,
One heart, one bed, two bosoms, and one troth.
Hermia.
Nay, good Lysander. For my sake, my dear,
Lie further off yet, do not lie so near.
Lysander.
O, take the sense,° sweet, of my innocence!   45
Love takes the meaning in love's conference.°
I mean, that my heart unto yours is knit,
So that but one heart we can make of it:
Two bosoms interchainèd with an oath;
So then two bosoms and a single troth.°   50
Then by your side no bed-room me deny,
For lying so, Hermia, I do not lie.°
Hermia.
Lysander riddles very prettily.
Now much beshrew° my manners and my pride,
If Hermia meant to say Lysander lied.   55
But, gentle friend, for love and courtesy
Lie further off, in human modesty.
Such separation as may well be said
Becomes a virtuous bachelor and a maid,
So far be distant; and, good night, sweet friend.   60
Thy love ne'er alter till thy sweet life end!

---

36. **troth:** truth.
45. **take the sense:** understand the meaning.
46. **Love ... conference:** lovers understand the meaning of each other's
    words.
50. **troth:** pledge of fidelity.
52. **lie:** tell an untruth; with a pun on *lie,* meaning "recline."
54. **beshrew:** curse, scold.

Lysander.
Amen, amen, to that fair prayer, say I,
And then end life when I end loyalty!
Here is my bed. Sleep give thee all his rest!
Hermia.
With half that wish the wisher's eyes be pressed! 65

They sleep.

Enter PUCK.

Puck.
Through the forest have I gone,
But Athenian found I none,
On whose eyes I might approve°
This flower's force in stirring love.
Night and silence.—Who is here?   70
Weeds° of Athens he doth wear:
This is he, my master said,
Despiséd the Athenian maid;
And here the maiden, sleeping sound,
On the dank and dirty ground.   75
Pretty soul! She durst not lie
Near this lack-love, this kill-courtesy.
Churl,° upon thy eyes I throw
All the power this charm doth owe.°
When thou wak'st, let love forbid   80
Sleep his seat on thy eyelid.
So awake when I am gone,
For I must now to Oberon.

Exit.

Enter DEMETRIUS *and* HELENA, *running.*

Helena.
Stay, though thou kill me, sweet Demetrius.

---

68. **approve:** try, test.
71. **Weeds:** clothing, garments.
78. **Churl:** crude fellow.
79. **owe:** own, possess.

Demetrius.

I charge thee, hence, and do not haunt me thus.　　85
Helena.

O, wilt thou darkling° leave me? Do not so.
Demetrius.

Stay, on thy peril! I alone will go.

Exit.

Helena.

O, I am out of breath in this fond chase!
The more my prayer, the lesser is my grace.
Happy is Hermia, wheresoe'er she lies,　　90
For she hath blessèd and attractive eyes.
How came her eyes so bright? Not with salt tears.
If so, my eyes are oft'ner washed than hers.
No, no, I am as ugly as a bear,
For beasts that meet me run away for fear.　　95
Therefore no marvel though Demetrius
Do, as a monster, fly my presence thus.
What wicked and dissembling glass of mine
Made me compare with Hermia's sphery eyne?°
But who is here? Lysander! On the ground!　　100
Dead? Or asleep? I see no blood, no wound.
Lysander, if you live, good sir, awake.
Lysander. [*Awaking.*]

And run through fire I will for thy sweet sake.
Transparent° Helena! Nature shows art,
That through thy bosom makes me see thy heart.　　105
Where is Demetrius? O, how fit a word
Is that vile name to perish on my sword!
Helena.

Do not say so, Lysander, say not so.

86.　**darkling:** in the dark.
99.　**sphery eyne:** eyes as bright as stars.
104.　**Transparent:** radiant; perhaps also meaning "capable of being
　　　seen through" or "ingenuous."

What though he love your Hermia? Lord, what
   though?
Yet Hermia still loves you. Then be content.   110
Lysander.
   Content with Hermia! No; I do repent
   The tedious minutes I with her have spent.
   Not Hermia but Helena I love:
   Who will not change a raven for a dove?
   The will of man is by his reason swayed   115
   And reason says you are the worthier maid.
   Things growing are not ripe until their season:
   So I, being young, till now ripe not to reason.
   And touching now the point of human skill,°
   Reason becomes the marshal to my will,   120
   And leads me to your eyes, where I o'erlook
   Love's stories, written in love's richest book.
Helena.
   Wherefore was I to this keen mockery born?
   When at your hands did I deserve this scorn?
   Is't not enough, is't not enough, young man,   125
   That I did never, no, nor never can,
   Deserve a sweet look from Demetrius' eye,
   But you must flout° my insufficiency?
   Good troth, you do me wrong, good sooth, you do,
   In such disdainful manner me to woo.   130
   But fare you well. Perforce I must confess
   I thought you lord of more true gentleness.°
   O, that a lady, of one man refused,
   Should of another therefore be abused!

                                    Exit.

Lysander.
   She sees not Hermia. Hermia, sleep thou there,   135
   And never mayst thou come Lysander near!

---

119. **touching ... skill:** now reaching the full use of reason.
128. **flout:** make fun of.
132. **gentleness:** nobility of character.

For as a surfeit of the sweetest things
The deepest loathing to the stomach brings,
Or as the heresies that men do leave
Are hated most of those they did deceive,   140
So thou, my surfeit and my heresy,
Of all be hated, but the most of me!
And, all my powers, address° your love and might
To honor Helen and to be her knight!

                                  Exit.

Hermia. [*Awaking.*]
Help me, Lysander, help me! Do thy best   145
To pluck this crawling serpent from my breast!
Ay me, for pity! What a dream was here!
Lysander, look how I do quake with fear.
Methought a serpent eat° my heart away,
And you sat smiling at his cruel prey.   150
Lysander! What, removed? Lysander! Lord!
What, out of hearing? Gone? No sound, no word?
Alack, where are you? Speak, an if° you hear;
Speak, of° all loves! I swoon almost with fear.
No? Then I well perceive you are not nigh.   155
Either death or you I'll find immediately.

                                  Exit.

---

143. address: direct.
149. eat: ate (pronounced "et").
153. an if: if.
154. of: on behalf of.

Act III

Scene 1. The wood. TITANIA *lying asleep.*

Enter QUINCE, SNUG, BOTTOM, FLUTE, SNOUT, *and*
STARVELING.

Bottom. Are we all met?

Quince. Pat,° pat; and here's a marvail's° convenient
place for our rehearsal. This green plot shall be
our stage, this hawthorn brake our tiring house,°
and we will do it in action as we will do it before   5
the duke.

Bottom. Peter Quince?

Quince. What sayest thou, bully° Bottom?

Bottom. There are things in this comedy of Pyramus
and Thisby that will never please. First, Pyramus   10
must draw a sword to kill himself; which the
ladies cannot abide. How answer you that?

Snout. By'r lakin,° a parlous° fear.

Starveling. I believe we must leave the killing out,
when all is done.   15

Bottom. Not a whit. I have a device to make all
well. Write me a prologue, and let the prologue
seem to say, we will do no harm with our swords,
and that Pyramus is not killed indeed; and, for the
more better assurance, tell them that I Pyramus   20
am not Pyramus, but Bottom the weaver. This

III.1.2. **Pat:** exactly. **marvail's:** Quince means *marvelous.*
4.   **tiring house:** dressing room.
8.   **bully:** jolly fellow.
13.   **By'r lakin:** interjection, "by Our Lady." **parlous:** perilous,
      terrible.

will put them out of fear.

Quince. Well, we will have such a prologue, and it
    shall be written in eight and six.°

Bottom. No, make it two more; let it be written in   25
    eight and eight.

Snout. Will not the ladies be afeard of the lion?

Starveling. I fear it, I promise you.

Bottom. Masters, you ought to consider with
    yourselves. To bring in—God shield us!—a lion   30
    among ladies, is a most dreadful thing. For there
    is not a more fearful wild fowl than your lion
    living; and we ought to look to't.

Snout. Therefore another prologue must tell he is not
    a lion.   35

Bottom. Nay, you must name his name, and half his
    face must be seen through the lion's neck, and he
    himself must speak through, saying thus, or to the
    same defect—"Ladies"—or, "Fair ladies—I
    would wish you"—or, "I would request you"—or,   40
    "I would entreat you—not to fear, not to tremble:
    my life for yours. If you think I come hither as a
    lion, it were pity of my life.° No, I am no such
    thing. I am a man as other men are." And there
    indeed let him name his name, and tell them   45
    plainly, he is Snug the joiner.

Quince. Well, it shall be so. But there is two hard
    things; that is, to bring the moonlight into a
    chamber; for, you know, Pyramus and Thisby meet
    by moonlight.   50

Snout. Doth the moon shine that night we play our
    play?

Bottom. A calendar, a calendar! Look in the almanac;
    find out moonshine, find out moonshine.

---

24.   **eight and six:** a common ballad measure consisting of
        alternating eight-syllable and six-syllable lines.
43.   **pity ... life:** a bad thing for me.

Quince. Yes, it doth shine that night.   55
Bottom. Why, then may you leave a casement of the
  great chamber window, where we play, open, and
  the moon may shine in at the casement.
  Quince. Ay; or else one must come in with a bush
  of thorns° and a lantern, and say he comes to   60
  disfigure,° or to present, the person of Moonshine.
  Then, there is another thing: we must have a wall
  in the great chamber; for Pyramus and Thisby, says
  the story, did talk through the chink of a wall.
Snout. You can never bring in a wall. What say you,   65
  Bottom?
Bottom. Some man or other must present Wall: and let
  him have some plaster, or some loam, or some
  roughcast° about him, to signify Wall; and let him
  hold his fingers thus, and through that cranny   70
  shall Pyramus and Thisby whisper.
Quince. If that may be, then all is well. Come, sit
  down, every mother's son, and rehearse your parts.
  Pyramus, you begin. When you have spoken your
  speech, enter into that brake; and so everyone   75
  according to his cue.

  Enter PUCK.

Puck.
  What hempen homespuns° have we swagg'ring
    here,
  So near the cradle of the Fairy Queen?
  What, a play toward!° I'll be an auditor;
  An actor too perhaps, if I see cause.   80
Quince. Speak, Pyramus. Thisby, stand forth.

59–60. bush of thorns: According to legend, the job of the man in the
    moon is to gather firewood on Sundays.
61.   **disfigure:** Quince means *figure* (represent).
69.   **roughcast:** plaster used on outside walls.
77.   **hempen homespuns:** country bumpkins dressed in coarse cloth
    made from hemp.
79.   **toward:** is about to take place.

Pyramus [Bottom].
  Thisby, the flowers of odious savors sweet—
Quince. Odors, odors.
Pyramus. —odors savors sweet:
      So hath thy breath, my dearest Thisby dear.   85
    But hark, a voice! Stay thou but here awhile,
      And by and by I will to thee appear.

                                                Exit.

Puck.
  A stranger Pyramus than e'er played here!

                                                Exit.

Thisby [Flute]. Must I speak now?
Quince. Ay, marry, must you. For you must understand   90
    he goes but to see a noise that he heard, and is to
    come again.
Thisby.
    Most radiant Pyramus, most lily-white of hue,
      Of color like the red rose on triumphant brier,
    Most brisky juvenal,° and eke° most lovely Jew,°   95
      As true as truest horse, that yet would never
          tire,
    I'll meet thee, Pyramus, at Ninny's° tomb.
Quince. "Ninus' tomb," man. Why, you must not speak
    that yet. That you answer to Pyramus. You speak
    all your part at once, cues and all. Pyramus,   100
    enter. Your cue is past; it is "never tire."
Thisby.
    O—as true as truest horse, that yet would never
        tire.

    Reenter PUCK, *and* BOTTOM *with an ass's head.*

---

95.   **brisky juvenal:** lively youth. **eke:** also. **Jew:** probably
       included for its alliterative effect with *juvenal.*
97.   **Ninny's:** Flute means *Ninus'.* Ninus was the legendary
       founder of the city of Nineveh.

Pyramus.
  If I were fair, Thisby, I were only thine.
Quince. O monstrous! O strange! We are haunted.
  Pray, masters! Fly, masters! Help!   105

Exeunt QUINCE, SNUG, FLUTE, SNOUT, *and* STARVELING.

Puck.
  I'll follow you, I'll lead you about a round,°
    Through bog, through bush, through brake,
      through brier.
  Sometime a horse I'll be, sometime a hound,
    A hog, a headless bear, sometime a fire;
  And neigh, and bark, and grunt, and roar,
    and burn,   110
  Like horse, hound, hog, bear, fire, at every turn.

                                               Exit.

Bottom. Why do they run away? This is a knavery
  of them to make me afeard.

Enter SNOUT.

Snout. O Bottom, thou art changed! What do I see
  on thee?   115
Bottom. What do you see? You see an ass head of
  your own, do you?

                                          Exit SNOUT.

Enter QUINCE.

Quince. Bless thee, Bottom! Bless thee! Thou art
  translated.°

                                               Exit.

Bottom. I see their knavery. This is to make an ass   120
  of me; to fright me, if they could. But I will not
  stir from this place, do what they can. I will

---

106. **about a round:** roundabout.
119. **translated:** changed utterly, transformed.

walk up and down here, and will sing, that they
shall hear I am not afraid.

Sings.

    The woosel° cock so black of hue,   125
        With orange-tawny bill,
    The throstle with his note so true,
        The wren with little quill°—
Titania. [*Awaking.*]
What angel wakes me from my flow'ry bed?
Bottom. [*Sings.*]
    The finch, the sparrow, and the lark,   130
        The plain-song cuckoo gray,
    Whose note full many a man doth mark,
        And dares not answer nay—
for, indeed, who would set his wit° to so foolish
a bird? Who would give a bird the lie,° though   135
he cry "cuckoo" never so?°
Titania.
I pray thee, gentle mortal, sing again:
Mine ear is much enamored of thy note;
So is mine eye enthrallèd to thy shape;
And thy fair virtue's force perforce doth move me 140
On the first view to say, to swear, I love thee.
Bottom. Methinks, mistress, you should have little
reason for that. And yet, to say the truth, reason
and love keep little company together nowadays;
the more the pity, that some honest neighbors   145
will not make them friends. Nay, I can gleek°
upon occasion.

---

125. **woosel:** ouzel, blackbird.
128. **quill:** literally, reed pipe; here meaning "piping song."
134. **set his wit:** use his intelligence to respond.
135. **give ... lie:** contradict a bird. The cuckoo's song supposedly
    marks a man as a cuckold, someone whose wife has been
    unfaithful.
136. **never so:** every so often.
146. **gleek:** scoff, jest satirically.

Titania.
Thou art as wise as thou art beautiful.
Bottom. Not so, neither; but if I had wit enough to
get out of this wood, I have enough to serve   150
mine own turn.
Titania.
Out of this wood do not desire to go.
Thou shalt remain here, whether thou wilt or no.
I am a spirit of no common rate.°
The summer still doth tend upon° my state;   155
And I do love thee. Therefore, go with me.
I'll give thee fairies to attend on thee,
And they shall fetch thee jewels from the deep,
And sing, while thou on pressèd flowers dost
sleep:
And I will purge thy mortal grossness so,   160
That thou shalt like an airy spirit go.
Peaseblossom! Cobweb! Moth!° And Mustardseed!

Enter four fairies [PEASEBLOSSOM, COBWEB, MOTH,
and MUSTARDSEED].

Peaseblossom. Ready.
Cobweb.
And I.
Moth.   And I.
Mustardseed.   And I.
All.   Where shall we go?
Titania.
Be kind and courteous to this gentleman;   165
Hop in his walks, and gambol in his eyes;
Feed him with apricocks and dewberries,
With purple grapes, green figs, and mulberries;
The honey bags steal from the humblebees,

---

154. **rate:** rank.
155. **still doth tend upon:** always waits upon.
162. **Moth:** pronounced "mote"; probably a speck (mote) rather
than an insect is meant.

And for night tapers crop their waxen thighs,   170
And light them at the fiery glowworm's eyes,
To have my love to bed and to arise;
And pluck the wings from painted butterflies,
To fan the moonbeams from his sleeping eyes.
Nod to him, elves, and do him courtesies.   175
Peaseblossom. Hail, mortal!
Cobweb. Hail!
Moth. Hail!
Mustardseed. Hail!
Bottom. I cry your worships mercy,° heartily: I   180
beseech your worship's name.
Cobweb. Cobweb.
Bottom. I shall desire you of more acquaintance,°
good Master Cobweb: if I cut my finger, I shall
make bold with you.° Your name, honest   185
gentleman?
Peaseblossom. Peaseblossom.
Bottom. I pray you, commend me to Mistress Squash,°
your mother, and to Master Peascod,° your father.
Good Master Peaseblossom, I shall desire you of   190
more acquaintance too. Your name, I beseech you,
sir?
Mustardseed. Mustardseed.
Bottom. Good Master Mustardseed, I know your
patience well. That same cowardly, giantlike   195
ox-beef hath devoured° many a gentleman of
your house. I promise you your kindred hath made
my eyes water ere now. I desire you of more
acquaintance, good Master Mustardseed.

---

180. I ... mercy: I beg pardon of your lordships.
183. I ... acquaintance: I desire to know you better.
184–185. if ... you: Cobwebs were used to stop the flow of blood.
188. Squash: unripe peapod.
189. Peascod: ripe peapod, in contrast to squash.
196. devoured: because beef is often flavored with mustard.

Titania.
> Come, wait upon him; lead him to my bower.   200
> The moon methinks looks with a wat'ry eye;
> And when she weeps, weeps every little flower,
> Lamenting some enforcèd° chastity.
> Tie up my lover's tongue, bring him silently.

Exeunt.

Scene 2. *Another part of the wood.*

Enter OBERON.

Oberon.
> I wonder if Titania be awaked;
> Then, what it was that next came in her eye,
> Which she must dote on in extremity.°

Enter PUCK.

> Here comes my messenger. How now, mad spirit!
> What night-rule° now about this haunted grove?   5

Puck.
> My mistress with a monster is in love.
> Near to her close° and consecrated bower,
> While she was in her dull and sleeping hour,
> A crew of patches,° rude mechanicals,°
> That work for bread upon Athenian stalls,   10
> Were met together to rehearse a play,
> Intended for great Theseus' nuptial day.
> The shallowest thickskin of that barren sort,°
> Who Pyramus presented in their sport,
> Forsook his scene, and entered in a brake.   15

---

203. enforcèd: violated.
III.2.3. in extremity: to the extreme.
5.   night-rule: happening during the night.
7.   close: private, secret.
9.   patches: clowns, fools. **rude mechanicals:** crude laborers.
13.   barren sort: stupid company.

When I did him at this advantage take,
An ass's nole° I fixèd on his head.
Anon° his Thisby must be answerèd,
And forth my mimic comes. When they him spy,
As wild geese that the creeping fowler eye,   20
Or russet-pated choughs, many in sort,°
Rising and cawing at the gun's report,
Sever themselves and madly sweep the sky,
So, at his sight, away his fellows fly;
And, at our stamp, here o'er and o'er one falls;   25
He murder cries, and help from Athens calls.
Their sense thus weak, lost with their fears
    thus strong,
Made senseless things begin to do them wrong;
For briers and thorns at their apparel snatch;
Some sleeves, some hats, from yielders all
    things catch.   30
I led them on in this distracted fear,
And left sweet Pyramus translated there:
When in that moment, so it came to pass,
Titania waked, and straightway loved an ass.

Oberon.

This falls out better than I could devise.   35
But hast thou yet latched° the Athenian's eyes
With the love juice, as I did bid thee do?

Puck.

I took him sleeping—that is finished too—
And the Athenian woman by his side;
That, when he waked, of force° she must be eyed.   40

Enter DEMETRIUS *and* HERMIA.

---

17.   **nole:** head, "noodle."
18.   **Anon:** soon, presently.
21.   **russet-pated ... sort:** gray-headed jackdaws in a flock.
36.   **latched:** probably meaning "moistened."
40.   **of force:** of necessity.

Oberon.

Stand close:° this is the same Athenian.

Puck.

This is the woman, but not this the man.

Demetrius.

O, why rebuke you him that loves you so?
Lay breath so bitter on your bitter foe.

Hermia.

Now I but chide; but I should use thee worse,   45
For thou, I fear, hast given me cause to curse.
If thou hast slain Lysander in his sleep,
Being o'er shoes in blood, plunge in the deep,
And kill me too.
The sun was not so true unto the day   50
As he to me. Would he have stolen away
From sleeping Hermia? I'll believe as soon
This whole° earth may be bored, and that the
    moon
May through the center creep, and so displease
Her brother's° noontide with th' Antipodes.°   55
It cannot be but thou hast murd'red him.
So should a murderer look, so dead,° so grim.

Demetrius.

So should the murdered look; and so should I,
Pierced through the heart with your stern cruelty.
Yet you, the murderer, look as bright, as clear,   60
As yonder Venus in her glimmering sphere.

Hermia.

What's this to my Lysander? Where is he?
Ah, good Demetrius, wilt thou give him me?

Demetrius.

I had rather give his carcass to my hounds.

---

41.   **Stand close:** hide, conceal yourself.
53.   **whole:** solid.
55.   **Her brother's:** the sun's. **Antipodes:** those who live on the
       other side of the earth.
57.   **dead:** deadly pale.

Hermia.

    Out, dog! Out, cur! Thou driv'st me past the bounds   65
    Of maiden's patience. Hast thou slain him, then?
    Henceforth be never numb'red among men!
    O, once tell true! Tell true, even for my sake!
    Durst thou have looked upon him being awake?
    And hast thou killed him sleeping? O brave
        touch!°   70
    Could not a worm, an adder, do so much?
    An adder did it; for with doubler tongue
    Than thine, thou serpent, never adder stung.

Demetrius.

    You spend your passion on a misprised mood:°
    I am not guilty of Lysander's blood;   75
    Nor is he dead, for aught that I can tell.

Hermia.

    I pray thee, tell me then that he is well.

Demetrius.

    An if I could, what should I get therefore?

Hermia.

    A privilege, never to see me more.
    And from thy hated presence part I so.   80
    See me no more, whether he be dead or no.

                                      Exit.

Demetrius.

    There is no following her in this fierce vein.
    Here therefore for a while I will remain.
    So sorrow's heaviness doth heavier grow
    For debt that bankrupt sleep doth sorrow owe;°   85
    Which now in some slight measure it will pay,
    If for his tender° here I make some stay.

    Lies down and sleeps.

---

70.   **brave touch:** splendid stroke; said ironically here.
74.   **misprised mood:** mistaken anger.
85.   **For ... owe:** because of sorrow's responsibility for much
      sleeplessness.
87.   **tender:** offer.

Oberon.

What hast thou done? Thou hast mistaken quite,
And laid the love juice on some truelove's sight.
Of thy misprision° must perforce ensue   90
Some true love turned, and not a false turned true.

Puck.

Then fate o'errules, that, one man holding troth,
A million fail, confounding oath on oath.°

Oberon.

About the wood go swifter than the wind,
And Helena of Athens look thou find.   95
All fancy-sick° she is and pale of cheer,°
With sighs of love, that costs the fresh blood
    dear:
By some illusion see thou bring her here.
I'll charm his eyes against she do appear.°

Puck.

I go, I go; look how I go,   100
Swifter than arrow from the Tartar's bow.

                                              Exit.

Oberon.

Flower of this purple dye,
Hit with Cupid's archery,
Sink in apple of his eye.
When his love he doth espy,   105
Let her shine as gloriously
As the Venus of the sky.
When thou wak'st, if she be by,
Beg of her for remedy.

Enter PUCK.

Puck.

Captain of our fairyband,   110

---

90. **misprision:** mistake.
93. **confounding ... oath:** breaking oath after oath.
96. **fancy-sick:** lovesick. **cheer:** face, look.
99. **against ... appear:** in preparation for her appearance.

>Helena is here at hand;
>And the youth, mistook by me,
>Pleading for a lover's fee.
>Shall we their fond pageant° see?
>Lord, what fools these mortals be!   115

Oberon.

>Stand aside. The noise they make
>Will cause Demetrius to awake.

Puck.

>Then will two at once woo one;
>That must needs be sport alone;°
>And those things do best please me   120
>That befall prepost'rously.

Enter LYSANDER *and* HELENA.

Lysander.

>Why should you think that I should woo in scorn?
>   Scorn and derision never come in tears:
>Look, when I vow, I weep; and vows so born,
>   In their nativity all truth appears.   125
>How can these things in me seem scorn to you,
>Bearing the badge of faith,° to prove them true?

Helena.

>You do advance° your cunning more and more.
>   When truth kills truth, O devilish-holy
>   fray!
>These vows are Hermia's: will you give her o'er?   130
>   Weigh oath with oath, and you will nothing
>   weigh.
>Your vows to her and me, put in two scales,
>Will even weigh; and both as light as tales.

Lysander.

>I had no judgment when to her I swore.

---

114. **fond pageant:** foolish show.
119. **alone:** unique, unparalleled.
127. **badge of faith:** Lysander is referring to his tears.
128. **advance:** display, put forward.

Helena.

Nor none, in my mind, now you give her o'er.   135

Lysander.

Demetrius loves her, and he loves not you.

Demetrius. [*Awaking.*]

O Helen, goddess, nymph, perfect, divine!
To what, my love, shall I compare thine eyne?
Crystal is muddy. O, how ripe in show
Thy lips, those kissing cherries, tempting grow!   140
That pure congealèd white, high Taurus'° snow,
Fanned with the eastern wind, turns to a crow
When thou hold'st up thy hand: O, let me kiss
This princess of pure white, this seal of bliss!

Helena.

O spite! O hell! I see you all are bent   145
To set against me for your merriment:
If you were civil and knew courtesy,
You would not do me thus much injury.
Can you not hate me, as I know you do,
But you must join in souls to mock me too?   150
If you were men, as men you are in show,
You would not use a gentle° lady so;
To vow, and swear, and superpraise my parts,°
When I am sure you hate me with your hearts.
You both are rivals, and love Hermia;   155
And now both rivals to mock Helena:
A trim° exploit, a manly enterprise,
To conjure tears up in a poor maid's eyes
With your derision! None of noble sort
Would so offend a virgin, and extort°   160
A poor soul's patience, all to make you sport.

---

141. **Taurus':** of the Taurus Mountains, in Turkey.
152. **gentle:** well-born.
153. **parts:** qualities.
157. **trim:** fine, splendid; used ironically here.
160. **extort:** wear out by torturing.

Lysander.
> You are unkind, Demetrius. Be not so;
> For you love Hermia; this you know I know.
> And here, with all good will, with all my heart,
> In Hermia's love I yield you up my part;   165
> And yours of Helena to me bequeath,
> Whom I do love, and will do till my death.

Helena.
> Never did mockers waste more idle breath.

Demetrius.
> Lysander, keep thy Hermia; I will none.
> If e'er I loved her, all that love is gone.   170
> My heart to her but as guestwise sojourned,
> And now to Helen is it home returned,
> There to remain.

Lysander.   Helen, it is not so.

Demetrius.
> Disparage not the faith thou dost not know,
> Lest, to thy peril, thou aby it dear.°   175
> Look, where thy love comes; yonder is thy dear.

Enter HERMIA.

Hermia.
> Dark night, that from the eye his° function takes,
> The ear more quick of apprehension makes;
> Wherein it doth impair the seeing sense,
> It pays the hearing double recompense.   180
> Thou art not by mine eye, Lysander, found;
> Mine ear, I thank it, brought me to thy sound.
> But why unkindly didst thou leave me so?

Lysander.
> Why should he stay, whom love doth press
>   to go?

Hermia.
> What love could press Lysander from my side?   185

---

175. **aby it dear:** pay dearly for it.
177. **his:** its (the eye's).

Lysander.
 Lysander's love, that would not let him bide,
 Fair Helena, who more engilds the night
 Than all yon fiery oes° and eyes of light.
 Why seek'st thou me? Could not this make thee
  know,
 The hate I bare thee made me leave thee so? 190
Hermia.
 You speak not as you think: it cannot be.
Helena.
 Lo, she is one of this confederacy!
 Now I perceive they have conjoined all three
 To fashion this false sport, in spite of me.
 Injurious° Hermia! Most ungrateful maid! 195
 Have you conspired, have you with these
  contrived
 To bait° me with this foul derision?
 Is all the counsel that we two have shared,
 The sister's vows, the hours that we have spent,
 When we have chid the hasty-footed time 200
 For parting us—O, is all forgot?
 All school days friendship, childhood innocence?
 We, Hermia, like two artificial° gods,
 Have with our needles created both one flower,
 Both on one sampler, sitting on one cushion, 205
 Both warbling of one song, both in one key;
 As if our hands, our sides, voices, and minds,
 Had been incorporate.° So we grew together,
 Like to a double cherry, seeming parted,
 But yet an union in partition; 210
 Two lovely berries molded on one stem;
 So, with two seeming bodies, but one heart;

---

188. **oes:** orbs; probably a pun on *eyes.*
195. **Injurious:** hurtful, insulting.
196–197. **contrived / To bait:** plotted to attack.
203. **artificial:** skilled in art.
208. **incorporate:** one body.

Two of the first, like coats in heraldry,
Due but to one, and crownèd with one crest.°
And will you rent° our ancient love asunder,   215
To join with men in scorning your poor friend?
It is not friendly, 'tis not maidenly.
Our sex, as well as I, may chide you for it,
Though I alone do feel the injury.

Hermia.
I am amazèd at your passionate words.   220
I scorn you not. It seems that you scorn me.

Helena.
Have you not set Lysander, as in scorn,
To follow me and praise my eyes and face?
And made your other love, Demetrius
(Who even but now did spurn me with his foot),   225
To call me goddess, nymph, divine and rare,
Precious, celestial? Wherefore speaks he this
To her he hates? And wherefore doth Lysander
Deny your love,° so rich within his soul,
And tender me (forsooth) affection,   230
But by your setting on, by your consent?
What though I be not so in grace as you,
So hung upon with love, so fortunate,
But miserable most, to love unloved?
This you should pity rather than despise.   235

Hermia.
I understand not what you mean by this.

Helena.
Ay, do! Persever,° counterfeit sad° looks,

213–214. **Two ... crest:** Helena appears to be imagining a shield
    with a coat of arms that appears twice but with a single
    crest, suggesting that she and Hermia have two bodies but
    one heart.
215. **rent:** tear.
229. **your love:** his love for you.
237. **Persever:** persevere (pronounced with the accent on the
    second syllable; rhymes with "forever"). **sad:** serious, grave.

Make mouths° upon me when I turn my back;
Wink each at other; hold the sweet jest up.
This sport, well carried, shall be chronicled.   240
If you have any pity, grace, or manners,
You would not make me such an argument.°
But fare ye well. 'Tis partly my own fault,
Which death or absence soon shall remedy.

Lysander.
　　Stay, gentle Helena; hear my excuse: 245
　　My love, my life, my soul, fair Helena!

Helena.
　　O excellent!

Hermia.　　　Sweet, do not scorn her so.

Demetrius.
　　If she cannot entreat,° I can compel.

Lysander.
　　Thou canst compel no more than she entreat.
　　Thy threats have no more strength than her
　　　　weak prayers.   250
　　Helen, I love thee; by my life, I do!
　　I swear by that which I will lose for thee,
　　To prove him false that says I love thee not.

Demetrius.
　　I say I love thee more than he can do.

Lysander.
　　If thou say so, withdraw and prove it too.   255

Demetrius.
　　Quick, come!

Hermia.　　　Lysander, whereto tends all this?

Lysander.
　　Away, you Ethiope!

Demetrius.　　　　　No, no; he'll
　　Seem to break loose; take on as you would follow,
　　But yet come not: you are a tame man, go!

---

238. **Make mouths:** make mocking faces.
242. **argument:** object of ridicule.
248. **entreat:** prevail by pleading.

Lysander.
    Hang off, thou cat, thou burr! Vile thing, let
      loose,   260
    Or I will shake thee from me like a serpent!
Hermia.
    Why are you grown so rude! What change is this,
    Sweet love?
Lysander.   Thy love! Out, tawny Tartar, out!
    Out, loathèd med'cine! O hated potion, hence!
Hermia.
    Do you not jest?
Helena.   Yes, sooth;° and so do you.   265
Lysander.
    Demetrius, I will keep my word° with thee.
Demetrius.
    I would I had your bond, for I perceive
    A weak bond holds you. I'll not trust your word.
Lysander.
    What, should I hurt her, strike her, kill her
      dead?
    Although I hate her, I'll not harm her so.   270
Hermia.
    What, can you do me greater harm than hate?
    Hate me! Wherefore? O me! What news, my love!
    Am not I Hermia? Are not you Lysander?
    I am as fair now as I was erewhile.
    Since night° you loved me; yet since night you
      left me.   275
    Why, then you left me—O, the gods forbid!—
    In earnest, shall I say?
Lysander.   Ay, by my life!
    And never did desire to see thee more.
    Therefore be out of hope, of question, of doubt;

---

265. **sooth:** truly.
266. **my word:** my pledge to fight with you.
275. **Since night:** since the beginning of this night.

Be certain, nothing truer. 'Tis no jest   280
That I do hate thee, and love Helena.

Hermia.

O me! You juggler! You canker blossom!°
You thief of love! What, have you come by night
And stol'n my love's heart from him?

Helena.   Fine, i'
faith!

Have you no modesty, no maiden shame,   285
No touch of bashfulness? What, will you tear
Impatient answers from my gentle tongue?
Fie, fie! You counterfeit, you puppet, you!

Hermia.

Puppet? Why so? Ay, that way goes the game.
Now I perceive that she hath made compare   290
Between our statures; she hath urged her height,
And with her personage, her tall personage,
Her height, forsooth, she hath prevailed with
    him.
And are you grown so high in his esteem,
Because I am so dwarfish and so low?   295
How low am I, thou painted maypole? Speak!
How low am I? I am not yet so low
But that my nails can reach unto thine eyes.

Helena.

I pray you, though you mock me, gentlemen,
Let her not hurt me. I was never curst;°   300
I have no gift at all in shrewishness;
I am a right maid° for my cowardice.
Let her not strike me. You perhaps may think,
Because she is something lower than myself,
That I can match her.

---

282. **canker blossom:** dog rose, or possibly canker worm that eats
     the blossom.
300. **curst:** quarrelsome.
302. **right maid:** true young woman.

Hermia.   Lower! Hark, again!   305
Helena.

Good Hermia, do not be so bitter with me.
I evermore did love you, Hermia,
Did ever keep your counsels, never wronged you;
Save that, in love unto Demetrius,
I told him of your stealth unto this wood.   310
He followed you; for love I followed him.
But he hath chid me hence, and threatened me
To strike me, spurn me, nay, to kill me too.
And now, so you will let me quiet go,
To Athens will I bear my folly back,   315
And follow you no further. Let me go.
You see how simple and how fond I am.

Hermia.

Why, get you gone. Who is't that hinders you?

Helena.

A foolish heart, that I leave here behind.

Hermia.

What, with Lysander?

Helena.   With Demetrius.   320

Lysander.

Be not afraid. She shall not harm thee, Helena.

Demetrius.

No, sir, she shall not, though you take her part.

Helena.

O, when she's angry, she is keen and shrewd!°
She was a vixen when she went to school;
And though she be but little, she is fierce.   325

Hermia.

"Little" again! Nothing but "low" and "little"!
Why will you suffer her to flout me thus?
Let me come to her.

Lysander.   Get you gone, you dwarf;

---

323. **keen and shrewd:** sharp-tongued and shrewish.

You minimus,° of hind'ring knotgrass° made;
You bead, you acorn!

Demetrius.   You are too officious   330
In her behalf that scorns your services.
Let her alone. Speak not of Helena;
Take not her part; for, if thou dost intend°
Never so little show of love to her,
Thou shalt aby° it.

Lysander.   Now she holds me not.   335
Now follow, if thou dar'st, to try whose right,
Of thine or mine, is most in Helena.

Demetrius.
Follow! Nay, I'll go with thee, cheek by jowl.

Exeunt LYSANDER *and* DEMETRIUS.

Hermia.
You, mistress, all this coil is 'long of you:°
Nay, go not back.

Helena.   I will not trust you, I,   340
Nor longer stay in your curst company.
Your hands than mine are quicker for a fray,
My legs are longer though, to run away.

Hermia.
I am amazed, and know not what to say.

Exeunt HELENA *and* HERMIA.

Oberon.
This is thy negligence. Still thou mistak'st,   345
Or else committ'st thy knaveries willfully.

Puck.
Believe me, king of shadows, I mistook.
Did not you tell me I should know the man

---

329. **minimus:** smallest thing. **knotgrass:** weed that was believed
to stunt children's growth.
333. **intend:** show, or possibly pretend.
335. **aby:** pay for.
339. **all ... you:** all this turmoil is brought on by you.

By the Athenian garments he had on?
And so far blameless proves my enterprise,   350
That I have 'nointed an Athenian's eyes;
And so far am I glad it so did sort,°
As this their jangling I esteem a sport.

Oberon.

Thou see'st these lovers seek a place to fight.
Hie therefore, Robin, overcast the night.   355
The starry welkin° cover thou anon
With drooping fog, as black as Acheron;°
And lead these testy° rivals so astray,
As° one come not within another's way.
Like to Lysander sometime frame thy tongue,   360
Then stir Demetrius up with bitter wrong;°
And sometime rail thou like Demetrius.
And from each other look thou lead them thus,
Till o'er their brows death-counterfeiting sleep
With leaden legs and batty wings doth creep.   365
Then crush this herb into Lysander's eye,
Whose liquor hath this virtuous° property,
To take from thence all error with his might,
And make his eyeballs roll with wonted sight.
When they next wake, all this derision°   370
Shall seem a dream and fruitless vision,
And back to Athens shall the lovers wend,
With league whose date° till death shall never
    end.
Whiles I in this affair do thee employ,

---

352. **sort:** turn out.
356. **welkin:** sky.
357. **Acheron:** one of the rivers of the underworld; here the word
     is used to suggest Hell.
358. **testy:** excited, irritable.
359. **As:** that.
361. **wrong:** insults.
367. **virtuous:** powerful.
370. **derision:** absurd delusion.
373. **With ... date:** in union whose term.

I'll to my queen and beg her Indian boy;   375
And then I will her charmèd eye release
From monster's view, and all things shall be
    peace.

Puck.

My fairy lord, this must be done with haste,
For night's swift dragons cut the clouds full fast,
And yonder shines Aurora's harbinger;°   380
At whose approach, ghosts, wand'ring here and
    there,
Troop home to churchyards: damnèd spirits all,
That in crossways and floods have burial,
Already to their wormy beds are gone.
For fear lest day should look their shames upon,   385
They willfully themselves exile from light,
And must for aye consort with black-browed night.

Oberon.

But we are spirits of another sort.
I with the morning's love° have oft made sport;
And, like a forester, the groves may tread,   390
Even till the eastern gate, all fiery-red,
Opening on Neptune with fair blessèd beams,
Turns into yellow gold his salt green streams.
But, notwithstanding, haste; make no delay.
We may effect this business yet ere day.   395

                        Exit

Puck.

    Up and down, up and down,
    I will lead them up and down:
    I am feared in field and town:
    Goblin,° lead them up and down.
Here comes one.   400

---

380. **Aurora's harbinger:** morning star, which announces dawn.
389. **the morning's love:** Aurora, the goddess of dawn, or possibly
    her lover, Cephalus.
399. **Goblin:** one of Puck's names (he is addressing himself).

Enter LYSANDER.

Lysander.
Where art thou, proud Demetrius? Speak thou
   now.
Puck.
Here, villain; drawn° and ready. Where art thou?
Lysander.
I will be with thee straight.
Puck.   Follow me, then,
To plainer° ground.

                       Exit LYSANDER.

Enter DEMETRIUS.

Demetrius.   Lysander! Speak again!
Thou runaway, thou coward, art thou fled?   405
Speak! In some bush? Where dost thou hide thy
   head?
Puck.
Thou coward, art thou bragging to the stars,
Telling the bushes that thou look'st for wars,
And wilt not come? Come, recreant! Come, thou
   child!
I'll whip thee with a rod. He is defiled   410
That draws a sword on thee.
Demetrius.   Yea, art thou there?
Puck.
Follow my voice. We'll try no manhood° here.

                       Exeunt.

Enter LYSANDER.

Lysander.
He goes before me and still dares me on:
When I come where he calls, then he is gone.
The villain is much lighter-heeled than I.   415

---

402. **drawn:** with drawn sword.
404. **plainer:** more level.
412. **try no manhood:** have no test of bravery.

I followed fast, but faster he did fly,
That fallen am I in dark uneven way,
And here will rest me. [*Lies down.*] Come, thou
　　gentle day!
For if but once thou show me thy gray light,
I'll find Demetrius, and revenge this spite.　　　　420

Sleeps.

Enter PUCK *and* DEMETRIUS.

Puck.
Ho, ho, ho! Coward, why com'st thou not?
Demetrius.
Abide me,° if thou dar'st; for well I wot°
Thou runn'st before me, shifting every place,
And dar'st not stand, nor look me in the face.
Where art thou now?
Puck.　　　　　　　Come hither. I am here.　　425
Demetrius.
Nay, then, thou mock'st me. Thou shalt buy this
　　dear,
If ever I thy face by daylight see.
Now, go thy way. Faintness constraineth me
To measure out my length on this cold bed.
By day's approach look to be visited.°　　　　430

Lies down and sleeps.

Enter HELENA.

Helena.
O weary night, O long and tedious night,
　　Abate° thy hours! Shine comforts from the
　　　　east,
That I may back to Athens by daylight,
　　From these that my poor company detest:

---

422. **Abide me:** face me. **wot:** know.
430. **look to be visited:** expect to be sought out.
432. **Abate:** shorten.

And sleep, that sometimes shuts up sorrow's eye, 435
Steal me awhile from mine own company.

Sleeps.

Puck.

> Yet but three? Come one more.
> Two of both kinds makes up four.
> Here she comes, curst° and sad:
> Cupid is a knavish lad, 440
> Thus to make poor females mad.

Enter HERMIA.

Hermia.

Never so weary, never so in woe;
> Bedabbled with the dew and torn with briers,
I can no further crawl, no further go;
> My legs can keep no pace with my desires. 445
Here will I rest me till the break of day.
Heavens shield Lysander, if they mean a fray!

Lies down and sleeps.

Puck.

> On the ground
> Sleep sound:
> I'll apply 450
> To your eye,
> Gentle lover, remedy.

Squeezing the juice on LYSANDER'*s eyes.*

> When thou wak'st,
> Thou tak'st
> True delight 455
> In the sight
> Of thy former lady's eye:
> And the country proverb known,

---

439. curst: bad-tempered.

That every man should take his own,
In your waking shall be shown.   460
    Jack shall have Jill;
    Nought shall go ill;
The man shall have his mare again,
    and all shall be well.

Exit.

Act IV

Scene 1. The woods. LYSANDER, DEMETRIUS, HELENA, *and*
HERMIA, *lying asleep.*

Enter TITANIA *and* BOTTOM; PEASEBLOSSOM, COBWEB,
MOTH, MUSTARDSEED, *and other* FAIRIES *attending;*
OBERON *behind, unseen.*

Titania.
 Come, sit thee down upon this flow'ry bed,
  While I thy amiable cheeks do coy,°
 And stick musk roses in thy sleek smooth head,
  And kiss thy fair large ears, my gentle joy.
Bottom. Where's Peaseblossom?   5
Peaseblossom. Ready.
Bottom. Scratch my head, Peaseblossom. Where's
 Mounsieur Cobweb?
Cobweb. Ready.
Bottom. Mounsieur Cobweb, good mounsieur, get you 10
 your weapons in your hand, and kill me a red-
 hipped humblebee on the top of a thistle; and,
 good mounsieur, bring me the honey bag. Do not
 fret yourself too much in the action, mounsieur;
 and, good mounsieur, have a care the honey bag 15
 break not; I would be loath to have you overflown
 with a honey bag, signior. Where's Mounsieur
 Mustardseed?
Mustardseed. Ready.
Bottom. Give me your neaf,° Mounsieur Mustardseed. 20

IV.1.2. **While ... coy:** while I caress your lovely cheeks.
20. **neaf:** fist, hand.

Pray you, leave your curtsy,° good mounsieur.
Mustardsccd. What's your will?
Bottom. Nothing, good mounsieur, but to help
    Cavalery° Cobweb to scratch. I must to the
    barber's, mounsieur; for methinks I am marvail's°   25
    hairy about the face; and I am such a tender ass,
    if my hair do but tickle me, I must scratch.
Titania.
    What, wilt thou hear some music, my sweet
      love?
Bottom. I have a reasonable good ear in music. Let's
    have the tongs and the bones.°   30
Titania.
    Or say, sweet love, what thou desirest to eat.
Bottom. Truly, a peck of provender. I could munch
    your good dry oats. Methinks I have a great desire
    to a bottle° of hay. Good hay, sweet hay, hath no
    fellow.   35
Titania.
    I have a venturous fairy that shall seek
    The squirrel's hoard, and fetch thee new nuts.
Bottom. I had rather have a handful or two of dried
    peas. But, I pray you, let none of your people stir
    me: I have an exposition of° sleep come upon me.   40
Titania.
    Sleep thou, and I will wind thee in my arms.
    Fairies, be gone, and be all ways away.

                        Exeunt FAIRIES.

So doth the woodbine the sweet honeysuckle

---

21.   **leave your curtsy:** stop bowing.
24.   **Cavalery:** Cavalier.
25.   **marvail's:** Bottom means *marvelous*.
30.   **tongs ... bones:** simple music made with metal tongs and bone
        clappers.
34.   **bottle:** bundle.
40.   **exposition of:** Bottom means *disposition for*.

Gently entwist; the female ivy° so
Enrings the barky fingers of the elm.   45
O, how I love thee! How I dote on thee!

They sleep.

Enter PUCK.

Oberon. [*Advancing.*]
Welcome, good Robin. See'st thou this sweet sight?
Her dotage now I do begin to pity:
For, meeting her of late behind the wood,
Seeking sweet favors° for this hateful fool,   50
I did upbraid her, and fall out with her.
For she his hairy temples then had rounded
With coronet of fresh and fragrant flowers;
And that same dew, which sometime° on the buds
Was wont° to swell, like round and orient° pearls,   55
Stood now within the pretty flouriets'° eyes,
Like tears, that did their own disgrace bewail.
When I had at my pleasure taunted her,
And she in mild terms begged my patience,
I then did ask of her her changeling child;   60
Which straight she gave me, and her fairy sent
To bear him to my bower in fairy land.
And now I have the boy, I will undo
This hateful imperfection of her eyes:
And, gentle Puck, take this transformèd scalp   65
From off the head of this Athenian swain,
That, he awaking when the other do,
May all to Athens back again repair,
And think no more of this night's accidents,°
But as the fierce vexation of a dream.   70

---

44.   **female ivy:** so called because it clings to the elm and is given
       support by it.
50.   **favors:** love tokens, probably flowers.
54.   **sometime:** in the past, formerly.
55.   **Was wont:** used to. **orient:** lustrous.
56.   **flouriets':** flowerets'.
69.   **accidents:** happenings.

But first I will release the Fairy Queen.
　　Be as thou wast wont to be;
　　See as thou wast wont to see.
　　Dian's bud o'er Cupid's flower
　　Hath such force and blessèd power.　　　　　75
Now, my Titania, wake you, my sweet queen.
Titania.
My Oberon, what visions have I seen!
Methought I was enamored of an ass.
Oberon.
There lies your love.
Titania.　　　　　　　How came these things
　　to pass?
O, how mine eyes do loathe his visage now!　　80
Oberon.
Silence awhile. Robin, take off this head.
Titania, music call; and strike more dead
Than common sleep of all these five the sense.
Titania.
Music, ho, music! Such as charmeth sleep!
Puck.
Now, when thou wak'st, with thine own fool's
　　eyes peep.　　　　　　　　　　　　　85
Oberon.
Sound, music! [*Music.*] Come, my queen, take
　　hands with me,
And rock the ground whereon these sleepers be.

Dance.

Now thou and I are new in amity,
And will tomorrow midnight solemnly°
Dance in Duke Theseus' house triumphantly,　　90
And bless it to all fair prosperity.
There shall the pairs of faithful lovers be
Wedded, with Theseus, all in jollity.

89.　**solemnly:** ceremoniously.

Puck.
> Fairy King, attend, and mark:
> I do hear the morning lark.   95

Oberon.
> Then, my queen, in silence sad,°
> Trip we after night's shade.
> We the globe can compass soon,
> Swifter than the wand'ring moon.

Titania.
> Come, my lord; and in our flight,   100
> Tell me how it came this night,
> That I sleeping here was found
> With these mortals on the ground.

>>>> *Exeunt.*

Horns winded within.
Enter THESEUS, HIPPOLYTA, EGEUS, *and train.*

Theseus.
> Go, one of you, find out the forester,
> For now our observation° is performed;   105
> And since we have the vaward° of the day,
> My love shall hear the music of my hounds.
> Uncouple in the western valley; let them go.
> Dispatch, I say, and find the forester.

>>>> *Exit an* ATTENDANT.

> We will, fair queen, up to the mountain's top,   110
> And mark the musical confusion
> Of hounds and echo in conjunction.

Hippolyta.
> I was with Hercules and Cadmus once,
> When in a wood of Crete they bayed the bear
> With hounds of Sparta. Never did I hear   115
> Such gallant chiding; for, besides the groves,

---

96. **sad:** sober, solemn.
105. **observation:** observance of the rite of May.
106. **vaward:** vanguard, here meaning "morning."

The skies, the fountains, every region near
Seemed all one mutual cry. I never heard
So musical a discord, such sweet thunder.

Theseus.

My hounds are bred out of the Spartan kind,   120
So flewed, so sanded;° and their heads are hung
With ears that sweep away the morning dew;
Crook-kneed, and dew-lapped like Thessalian
    bulls;
Slow in pursuit, but matched in mouth like bells,
Each under each.° A cry° more tunable   125
Was never holloed to, nor cheered with horn,
In Crete, in Sparta, nor in Thessaly.
Judge when you hear. But, soft!° What nymphs
    are these?

Egeus.

My lord, this is my daughter here asleep;
And this, Lysander; this Demetrius is;   130
This Helena, old Nedar's Helena:
I wonder of their being here together.

Theseus.

No doubt they rose up early to observe
The rite of May; and, hearing our intent,
Came here in grace of our solemnity.°   135
But speak, Egeus. Is not this the day
That Hermia should give answer of her choice?

Egeus.

It is, my lord.

Theseus.

Go, bid the huntsmen wake them with
    their horns.

---

121. **So ... sanded:** like Spartan hounds, with hanging cheeks and
    sandy color.
125. **Each under each:** of different tones, like a set of bells. **cry:** pack
    of hounds.
128. **soft:** wait.
135. **in ... solemnity:** in honor of our wedding.

Horns and shout within. LYSANDER, DEMETRIUS,
HELENA, *and* HERMIA *wake and start up.*

Good morrow, friends. Saint Valentine is past: 140
Begin these wood birds but to couple now?°
Lysander.
Pardon, my lord.
Theseus.   I pray you all, stand up.
I know you two are rival enemies.
How comes this gentle concord in the world,
That hatred is so far from jealousy,°   145
To sleep by hate, and fear no enmity?
Lysander.
My lord, I shall reply amazedly,
Half sleep, half waking: but as yet, I swear,
I cannot truly say how I came here.
But, as I think—for truly would I speak,   150
And now I do bethink me, so it is—
I came with Hermia hither. Our intent
Was to be gone from Athens, where we might,
Without° the peril of the Athenian law—
Egeus.
Enough, enough, my lord; you have enough.   155
I beg the law, the law, upon his head.
They would have stol'n away; they would,
     Demetrius,
Thereby to have defeated° you and me,
You of your wife and me of my consent,
Of my consent that she should be your wife.   160
Demetrius.
My lord, fair Helen told me of their stealth,°
Of this their purpose hither to this wood,

---

141. **Begin ... now:** It was believed that birds begin mating on Saint
     Valentine's Day, February 14.
145. **jealousy:** suspicion.
154. **Without:** beyond, outside of.
158. **defeated:** cheated.
161. **stealth:** stealthy flight.

And I in fury hither followed them,
Fair Helena in fancy° following me.
But, my good lord, I wot not by what power—   165
But by some power it is—my love to Hermia,
Melted as the snow, seems to me now
As the remembrance of an idle gaud,°
Which in my childhood I did dote upon;
And all the faith, the virtue of my heart,   170
The object and the pleasure of mine eye,
Is only Helena. To her, my lord,
Was I betrothed ere I saw Hermia:
But, like a sickness, did I loathe this food;
But, as in health, come to my natural taste,   175
Now I do wish it, love it, long for it,
And will for evermore be true to it.

Theseus.
Fair lovers, you are fortunately met.
Of this discourse we more will hear anon.
Egeus, I will overbear your will,   180
For in the temple, by and by, with us
These couples shall eternally be knit;
And, for the morning now is something worn,°
Our purposed hunting shall be set aside.
Away with us to Athens! Three and three,   185
We'll hold a feast in great solemnity.
Come, Hippolyta.

    Exeunt THESEUS, HIPPOLYTA, EGEUS, *and train.*

Demetrius.
These things seem small and undistinguishable,
Like far-off mountains turnèd into clouds.

Hermia.
Methinks I see these things with parted eye,°   190
When everything seems double.

---

164. **in fancy:** in love.
168. **idle gaud:** worthless trinket.
183. **something worn:** somewhat spent; almost gone.
190. **with parted eye:** with the eyes unfocused.

Helena.   So methinks:
  And I have found Demetrius like a jewel,
  Mine own, and not mine own.
Demetrius.   Are you sure
  That we are awake? It seems to me
  That yet we sleep, we dream. Do not you think   195
  The duke was here, and bid us follow him?
Hermia.
  Yea, and my father.
Helena.   And Hippolyta.
Lysander.
  And he did bid us follow to the temple.
Demetrius.
  Why, then, we are awake. Let's follow him,
  And by the way let us recount our dreams.   200

                                        Exeunt.

Bottom. [*Awaking.*] When my cue comes, call me,
  and I will answer. My next is, "Most fair Pyramus."
  Heigh-ho! Peter Quince? Flute, the bellows
  mender? Snout, the tinker? Starveling? God's my
  life,° stol'n hence, and left me asleep? I have had   205
  a most rare vision. I have had a dream, past the
  wit of man to say what dream it was. Man is but
  an ass, if he go about to expound this dream.
  Methought I was—there is no man can tell what.
  Methought I was—and methought I had—but   210
  man is but a patched° fool if he will offer to say
  what methought I had. The eye of man hath not
  heard, the ear of man hath not seen, man's hand
  is not able to taste, his tongue to conceive, nor his
  heart to report,° what my dream was. I will get   215

204–205. God's my life: a common oath, possibly a shortened form of
  "God bless my life."
211.   patched: referring to the patchwork clothing worn by jesters.
212–215. The eye … report: Bottom's garbled version of I Corinthians
  2:9.

Peter Quince to write a ballet° of this dream. It
shall be called "Bottom's Dream," because it hath
no bottom; and I will sing it in the latter end of
a play, before the duke. Peradventure to make
it the more gracious, I shall sing it at her death.°   220

Exit.

Scene 2. *Athens. Quince's house.*

Enter QUINCE, FLUTE, SNOUT, *and* STARVELING.

Quince. Have you sent to Bottom's house? Is he
come home yet?
Starveling. He cannot be heard of. Out of doubt he
is transported.°
Flute. If he come not, then the play is marred. It   5
goes not forward, doth it?
Quince. It is not possible. You have not a man in all
Athens able to discharge° Pyramus but he.
Flute. No, he hath simply the best wit of any
handicraft man in Athens.   10
Quince. Yea, and the best person too; and he is a very
paramour for a sweet voice.
Flute. You must say "paragon." A paramour is, God
bless us, a thing of nought.°

Enter SNUG.

Snug. Masters, the duke is coming from the temple,   15
and there is two or three lords and ladies more
married. If our sport had gone forward, we had
all been made men.°
Flute. O sweet bully Bottom! Thus hath he lost

---

216. **ballet:** ballad.
220. **her death:** Thisby's death in the play.
4.   **transported:** carried off by the fairies.
8.   **discharge:** play, perform.
14.   **thing of nought:** wicked or shameful thing.
18.   **made men:** men whose fortunes are made.

sixpence a day° during his life. He could not have   20
scaped sixpence a day. An the duke had not given
him sixpence a day for playing Pyramus, I'll be
hanged. He would have deserved it. Sixpence a
day in Pyramus, or nothing.

Enter BOTTOM.

Bottom. Where are these lads? Where are these   25
hearts?
Quince. Bottom! O most courageous° day! O most
happy hour!
Bottom. Masters, I am to discourse wonders: but ask
me not what; for if I tell you, I am not true   30
Athenian. I will tell you everything, right as it
fell out.
Quince. Let us hear, sweet Bottom.
Bottom. Not a word of me.° All that I will tell you
is, that the duke hath dined. Get your apparel   35
together, good strings to your beards, new ribbons
to your pumps; meet presently at the palace;
every man look o'er his part; for the short and the
long is, our play is preferred.° In any case, let
Thisby have clean linen; and let not him that   40
plays the lion pare his nails, for they shall hang
out for the lion's claws. And, most dear actors, eat
no onions nor garlic, for we are to utter sweet
breath, and I do not doubt but to hear them say
it is a sweet comedy. No more words. Away!   45
Go, away!

Exeunt.

---

20.   **sixpence a day:** a pension from the duke.
27.   **courageous:** splendid, fine.
34.   **of me:** from me.
39.   **preferred:** put forward, recommended.

Act V

Scene 1. Athens. The palace of Theseus.

Enter THESEUS, HIPPOLYTA, PHILOSTRATE, LORDS, *and* ATTENDANTS.

Hippolyta.
'Tis strange, my Theseus, that these lovers speak of.
Theseus.
More strange than true. I never may believe
These antique° fables, nor these fairy toys.°
Lovers and madmen have such seething brains,
Such shaping fantasies, that apprehend   5
More than cool reason ever comprehends.
The lunatic, the lover, and the poet
Are of imagination all compact.°
One sees more devils than vast hell can hold,
That is the madman. The lover, all as frantic,   10
Sees Helen's beauty in a brow of Egypt.°
The poet's eye, in a fine frenzy rolling,
Doth glance from heaven to earth, from earth to
    heaven;
And as imagination bodies forth
The forms of things unknown, the poet's pen   15
Turns them to shapes, and gives to airy nothing
A local habitation and a name.
Such tricks hath strong imagination,
That, if it would but apprehend some joy,

V.1.3. **antique:** ancient, with a possible pun on *antic.* **toys:** trifles.
8.   **compact:** composed.
11.   **brow of Egypt:** face of a Gypsy.

73

It comprehends some bringer of that joy;° 20
Or in the night, imagining some fear,
How easy is a bush supposed a bear!
Hippolyta.
But all the story of the night told over,
And all their minds transfigured so together,
More witnesseth than fancy's images, 25
And grows to something of great constancy;°
But, howsoever, strange and admirable.°

Enter LYSANDER, DEMETRIUS, HERMIA, *and* HELENA.

Theseus.
Here come the lovers, full of joy and mirth.
Joy, gentle friends! Joy and fresh days of love
Accompany your hearts!
Lysander.   More than to us 30
Wait in your royal walks, your board, your bed!
Theseus.
Come now, what masques,° what dances shall we
    have,
To wear away this long age of three hours
Between our aftersupper and bedtime?
Where is our usual manager of mirth? 35
What revels are in hand? Is there no play,
To ease the anguish of a torturing hour?
Call Philostrate.
Philostrate.   Here, mighty Theseus.
Theseus.
Say, what abridgment° have you for this evening?
What masque? What music? How shall we
    beguile 40
The lazy time, if not with some delight?

---

20. It ... joy: it includes an imagined bringer of joy.
26. constancy: consistency, reality.
27. admirable: wonderful.
32. masques: balls or entertainments for masked dancers.
39. abridgment: entertainment or interlude that helps pass time.

Philostrate.

There is a brief° how many sports are ripe:°
Make choice of which your highness will see first.

Gives a paper.

Theseus. [*Reads.*]

"The battle with the centaurs, to be sung
By an Athenian eunuch to the harp."   45
We'll none of that. That have I told my love,
In glory of my kinsman Hercules.
"The riot of the tipsy Bacchanals,
Tearing the Thracian singer° in their rage."
That is an old device;° and it was played   50
When I from Thebes came last a conqueror.
"The thrice three Muses mourning for the death
Of learning, late deceased in beggary."
That is some satire, keen and critical,
Not sorting with° a nuptial ceremony.   55
"A tedious brief scene of young Pyramus
And his love Thisby; very tragical mirth."
Merry and tragical? Tedious and brief?
That is, hot ice and wondrous strange snow.
How shall we find the concord of this discord?   60

Philostrate.

A play there is, my lord, some ten words long,
Which is as brief as I have known a play;
But by ten words, my lord, it is too long,
Which makes it tedious. For in all the play
There is not one word apt, one player fitted.   65
And tragical, my noble lord, it is,
For Pyramus therein doth kill himself.
Which, when I saw rehearsed, I must confess,
Made mine eyes water; but more merry tears
The passion of loud laughter never shed.   70

---

42.   **brief:** written list. **ripe:** ready to be presented.
49.   **Thracian singer:** Orpheus.
50.   **device:** show.
55.   **sorting with:** suited to.

Theseus.
What are they that do play it?
Philostrate.
Hard-handed men, that work in Athens here,
Which never labored in their minds till now;
And now have toiled their unbreathed° memories
With this same play, against° your nuptial.   75
Theseus.
And we will hear it.
Philostrate.   No, my noble lord;
It is not for you. I have heard it over,
And it is nothing, nothing in the world;
Unless you can find sport in their intents,
Extremely stretched and conned with cruel pain,   80
To do you service.
Theseus.   I will hear that play;
For never anything can be amiss,
When simpleness and duty tender it.
Go, bring them in: and take your places, ladies.

                        Exit PHILOSTRATE.

Hippolyta.
I love not to see wretchedness o'ercharged,°   85
And duty in his service perishing.
Theseus.
Why, gentle sweet, you shall see no such thing.
Hippolyta.
He says they can do nothing in this kind.°
Theseus.
The kinder we, to give them thanks for nothing.
Our sport shall be to take what they mistake: 90
And what poor duty cannot do, noble respect
Takes it in might,° not merit.

---

74.   **unbreathed:** unexercised.
75.   **against:** in preparation for.
85.   **wretchedness o'ercharged:** poor people overburdened.
88.   **in this kind:** of this kind of thing (acting).
92.   **Takes ... might:** considers the ability and the effort made.

Where I have come, great clerks° have purposèd
To greet me with premeditated welcomes;
Where I have seen them shiver and look pale,   95
Make periods in the midst of sentences,
Throttle their practiced accent in their fears,
And, in conclusion, dumbly have broke off,
Not paying me a welcome. Trust me, sweet,
Out of this silence yet I picked a welcome;   100
And in the modesty of fearful duty
I read as much as from the rattling tongue
Of saucy and audacious eloquence.
Love, therefore, and tongue-tied simplicity
In least speak most, to my capacity.   105

Enter PHILOSTRATE.

Philostrate.
So please your grace, the Prologue is addressed.°
Theseus.
Let him approach.

Flourish of trumpets. Enter QUINCE *for the* PROLOGUE.

Prologue.
If we offend, it is with our good will.
    That you should think, we come not to offend,
But with good will. To show our simple skill,   110
    That is the true beginning of our end.°
Consider, then, we come but in despite.
    We do not come, as minding to content you,
Our true intent is. All for your delight,
    We are not here. That you should here repent
        you,   115
The actors are at hand; and, by their show,°
You shall know all, that you are like to know.

---

93. **clerks:** scholars.
106. **addressed:** ready.
111. **end:** aim.
116. **show:** probably means a "dumb show," or pantomime, that will
     follow.

Theseus. This fellow doth not stand upon points.°
Lysander. He hath rid his prologue like a rough
    colt; he knows not the stop. A good moral, my   120
    lord: it is not enough to speak, but to speak true.
Hippolyta. Indeed he hath played on this prologue
    like a child on a recorder; a sound, but not in
    government.°
Theseus. His speech was like a tangled chain;   125
    nothing impaired, but all disordered. Who is next?

Enter PYRAMUS *and* THISBY, WALL, MOONSHINE, *and*
LION.

Prologue.
    Gentles, perchance you wonder at this show;
        But wonder on, till truth make all things plain.
    This man is Pyramus, if you would know;
        This beauteous lady Thisby is certain.   130
    This man, with lime and roughcast, doth present
        Wall, that vile Wall which did these lovers
            sunder;
    And through Wall's chink, poor souls, they are
        content
        To whisper. At the which let no man wonder.
    This man, with lantern, dog, and bush of thorn,   135
        Presenteth Moonshine; for, if you will know,
    By moonshine did these lovers think no scorn
        To meet at Ninus' tomb, there, there to woo.
    This grisly beast, which Lion hight° by name,
    The trusty Thisby, coming first by night,   140
    Did scare away, or rather did affright;
    And, as she fled, her mantle she did fall,°
        Which Lion vile with bloody mouth did stain.

---

118. **stand upon points:** care about the rules of punctuation or other
      fine points.
124. **government:** control.
139. **hight:** is called.
142. **fall:** let drop.

Anon comes Pyramus, sweet youth and tall,°
    And finds his trusty Thisby's mantle slain: 145
Whereat, with blade, with bloody blameful
    blade,
    He bravely broached° his boiling bloody
        breast;
And Thisby, tarrying in mulberry shade,
    His dagger drew, and died. For all the rest,
Let Lion, Moonshine, Wall, and lovers twain   150
    At large discourse, while here they do remain.
Theseus. I wonder if the lion be to speak.
Demetrius. No wonder, my lord. One lion may, when
many asses do.

           Exeunt THISBY, LION, *and* MOONSHINE.

Wall.

In this same interlude it doth befall   155
That I, one Snout by name, present a wall;
And such a wall, as I would have you think,
That had in it a crannied hole or chink,
Through which the lovers, Pyramus and Thisby,
Did whisper often very secretly.   160
This loam, this roughcast, and this stone, doth
    show
That I am that same wall; the truth is so;
And this the cranny is, right and sinister,°
Through which the fearful lovers are to whisper.
Theseus. Would you desire lime and hair to speak   165
better?
Demetrius. It is the wittiest partition° that ever I
heard discourse, my lord.

Enter PYRAMUS.

---

144. **tall:** brave, stalwart.
147. **broached:** stabbed.
163. **right and sinister:** running from right to left.
167. **wittiest partition:** most intelligent wall; a pun on *partition,*
    which also means "section of a book or of a speech."

Theseus. Pyramus draws near the wall. Silence!
Pyramus.
> O grim-looked night! O night with hue so black!   170
> > O night, which ever art when day is not!
> O night, O night! Alack, alack, alack,
> > I fear my Thisby's promise is forgot!
> And thou, O wall, O sweet, O lovely wall,
> That stand'st between her father's ground
> > and mine!   175
> Thou wall, O wall, O sweet and lovely wall,
> > Show me thy chink, to blink through with
> > > mine eyne!

WALL *holds up his fingers.*

> Thanks, courteous wall. Jove shield thee well for
> > this!
> > But what see I? No Thisby do I see.
> O wicked wall, through whom I see no bliss!   180
> > Cursed be thy stones for thus deceiving me!

Theseus. The wall, methinks, being sensible,°
should curse again.°
Pyramus. No, in truth, sir, he should not. "Deceiving
me" is Thisby's cue. She is to enter now, and I am   185
to spy her through the wall. You shall see it will
fall pat as I told you. Yonder she comes.

Enter THISBY.

Thisby.
> O wall, full often hast thou heard my moans,
> > For parting my fair Pyramus and me!
> My cherry lips have often kissed thy stones,   190
> > Thy stones with lime and hair knit up in thee.
Pyramus.
> I see a voice: now will I to the chink,
> > To spy an I can hear my Thisby's face.
> Thisby!

---

182. **sensible:** aware, conscious.
183. **again:** in response.

Thisby. My love thou art, my love I think.

Pyramus.

Think what thou wilt, I am thy lover's grace;°   195
And, like Limander,° am I trusty still.

Thisby.

And I like Helen,° till the Fates me kill.

Pyramus.

Not Shafalus to Procrus° was so true.

Thisby.

As Shafalus to Procrus, I to you.

Pyramus.

O kiss me through the hole of this vile wall!   200

Thisby.

I kiss the wall's hole, not your lips at all.

Pyramus.

Wilt thou at Ninny's tomb meet me straightway?

Thisby.

'Tide life, 'tide death,° I come without delay.

Exeunt PYRAMUS *and* THISBY.

Wall.

Thus have I, Wall, my part dischargèd so;
And, being done, thus wall away doth go.   205

Exit.

Theseus. Now is the moon used between the two
neighbors.

Demetrius. No remedy, my lord, when walls are
so willful to hear without warning.°

---

195. **thy lover's grace:** thy gracious lover.
196. **Limander:** Bottom means Leander, but blends his name with Alexander.
197. **Helen:** Bottom probably means Hero, lover of Leander.
198. **Shafalus to Procrus:** Bottom means Cephalus and Procris, another pair of tragic lovers.
203. **'Tide ... death:** come life, come death.
208–209. **when ... warning:** when walls are so eager to listen without warning parents.

Hippolyta. This is the silliest stuff that ever I 210
heard.

Theseus. The best in this kind° are but shadows; and
the worst are no worse, if imagination amend them.

Hippolyta. It must be your imagination then, and
not theirs. 215

Theseus. If we imagine no worse of them than they
of themselves, they may pass for excellent men.
Here come two noble beasts in, a man and a lion.

Enter LION *and* MOONSHINE.

Lion.
You, ladies, you, whose gentle hearts do fear
    The smallest monstrous mouse that creeps on
        floor, 220
May now perchance both quake and tremble here,
    When lion rough in wildest rage doth roar.
Then know that I, as Snug the joiner, am
A lion fell,° nor else no lion's dam;
For, if I should as lion come in strife 225
Into this place, 'twere pity on my life.°

Theseus. A very gentle beast, and of a good conscience.

Demetrius. The very best at a beast, my lord, that
e'er I saw.

Lysander. This lion is a very fox for his valor. 230

Theseus. True; and a goose for his discretion.

Demetrius. Not so, my lord; for his valor cannot
carry his discretion, and the fox carries the
goose.

Theseus. His discretion, I am sure, cannot carry° 235
his valor; for the goose carries not the fox. It is
well. Leave it to his discretion, and let us listen
to the moon.

---

212. **in this kind:** of this sort, meaning plays or players.
224. **lion fell:** fierce lion, perhaps with a pun on *fell,* meaning "skin."
226. **pity on my life:** a dangerous thing for me.
235. **carry:** overcome, carry away.

Moonshine.
This lanthorn° doth the hornèd moon present—
Demetrius. He should have worn the horns on his   240
head.°
Theseus. He is no crescent, and his horns are invisible
within the circumference.
Moonshine.
This lanthorn doth the hornèd moon present,
Myself the man i' th' moon do seem to be.   245
Theseus. This is the greatest error of all the rest.
The man should be put into the lanthorn. How is
it else the man i' th' moon?
Demetrius. He dares not come there for the candle;
for, you see, it is already in snuff.°   250
Hippolyta. I am aweary of this moon. Would he
would change!
Theseus. It appears, by his small light of discretion,
that he is in the wane; but yet, in courtesy, in all
reason, we must stay the time.   255
Lysander. Proceed, Moon.
Moonshine. All that I have to say is to tell you that
the lanthorn is the moon; I, the man i' th' moon;
this thorn bush, my thorn bush; and this dog, my
dog.   260
Demetrius. Why, all these should be in the
lanthorn; for all these are in the moon. But,
silence! Here comes Thisby.

Enter THISBY.

Thisby.
This is old Ninny's tomb. Where is my love?
Lion. [*Roaring.*] Oh—   265

---

239. **lanthorn:** This spelling of *lantern* probably derives from the fact
that lanterns were commonly made of horn.
240–241. **horns ... head:** Cuckolds, deceived husbands, were said to
have horns.
250. **in snuff:** offended.

THISBY *runs off.*

Demetrius. Well roared, Lion.
Theseus. Well run, Thisby.
Hippolyta. Well shone, Moon. Truly, the moon
shines with a good grace.

The LION *shakes* THISBY's *mantle, and exit.*

Theseus. Well moused,° Lion.   270
Demetrius. And then came Pyramus.
Lysander. And so the lion vanished.

Enter PYRAMUS.

Pyramus.
   Sweet Moon, I thank thee for thy sunny beams;
      I thank thee, Moon, for shining now so bright;
   For, by thy gracious, golden, glittering gleams,   275
      I trust to take of truest Thisby sight.
            But stay, O spite!°
            But mark, poor knight,
      What dreadful dole° is here!
            Eyes, do you see?   280
            How can it be?
      O dainty duck! O dear!
            Thy mantle good,
            What, stained with blood!
      Approach, ye Furies fell!°   285
            O Fates, come, come,
            Cut thread and thrum;°
      Quail,° crush, conclude, and quell!°
Theseus. This passion, and the death of a dear
   friend, would go near to make a man look sad.   290

---

270. **moused:** shaken (like a mouse).
277. **spite:** ill fortune.
279. **dole:** sorrowful event.
285. **fell:** fierce.
287. **thread and thrum:** everything.
288. **Quail:** destroy. **quell:** kill.

Hippolyta. Beshrew my heart, but I pity the man.
Pyramus.
    O wherefore, nature, didst thou lions frame?
      Since lion vile hath here deflow'red my dear:
    Which is—no, no—which was the fairest dame
      That lived, that loved, that liked, that
        looked with cheer.°   295
              Come, tears, confound;
              Out, sword, and wound
          The pap of Pyramus;
              Ay, that left pap,
              Where heart doth hop.   300

Stabs himself.

         Thus die I, thus, thus, thus.
           Now am I dead,
           Now am I fled;
         My soul is in the sky,
            Tongue, lose thy light;   305
           Moon, take thy flight.

                     Exit MOONSHINE.

    Now die, die, die, die, die.

                         Dies.

Demetrius. No die, but an ace,° for him; for he is
    but one.
Lysander. Less than an ace, man; for he is dead, he   310
    is nothing.
Theseus. With the help of a surgeon he might yet
    recover, and yet prove an ass.
Hippolyta. How chance Moonshine is gone before
    Thisby comes back and finds her lover?   315
Theseus. She will find him by starlight. Here she
    comes; and her passion° ends the play.

---

295. cheer: countenance.
308. ace: the one-spot on a die.
317. passion: emotional speech.

Enter THISBY.

Hippolyta. Methinks she should not use a long one
for such a Pyramus. I hope she will be brief.

Demetrius. A mote will turn the balance, which   320
Pyramus, which Thisby, is the better; he for a
man, God warr'nt us; she for a woman, God
bless us!

Lysander. She hath spied him already with those
sweet eyes.   325

Demetrius. And thus she means,° videlicet:

Thisby.
      Asleep, my love?
        What, dead, my dove?
      O Pyramus, arise!
        Speak, speak. Quite dumb?   330
        Dead, dead? A tomb
      Must cover thy sweet eyes.
        These lily lips,
        This cherry nose,
      These yellow cowslip cheeks,   335
        Are gone, are gone.
        Lovers, make moan.
      His eyes were green as leeks.
        O Sisters Three,°
        Come, come to me,   340
      With hands as pale as milk;
        Lay them in gore,
        Since you have shore°
      With shears his thread of silk.
        Tongue, not a word.   345
        Come, trusty sword,
    Come, blade, my breast imbrue!°

   Stabs herself.

---

326. **means:** moans, laments.
339. **Sisters Three:** three Fates.
343. **shore:** shorn.
347. **imbrue:** stain with blood.

And, farewell, friends.
Thus Thisby ends.
Adieu, adieu, adieu.   350

Dies.

Theseus. Moonshine and Lion are left to bury the
dead.
Demetrius. Ay, and Wall too.
Bottom. [*Starting up.*] No, I assure you; the wall is
down that parted their fathers. Will it please   355
you to see the epilogue, or to hear a Bergomask
dance° between two of our company?
Theseus. No epilogue, I pray you; for your play
needs no excuse. Never excuse, for when the
players are all dead, there need none to be   360
blamed. Marry, if he that writ it had played
Pyramus and hanged himself in Thisby's garter,
it would have been a fine tragedy: and so it is,
truly; and very notably discharged. But, come,
your Bergomask. Let your epilogue alone.   365

A dance.

The iron tongue of midnight hath told° twelve.
Lovers, to bed; 'tis almost fairy time.
I fear we shall outsleep the coming morn,
As much as we this night have overwatched.
This palpable-gross° play hath well beguiled   370
The heavy gait of night. Sweet friends, to bed.
A fortnight hold we this solemnity,
In nightly revels and new jollity.

Exeunt.

Enter PUCK.

Puck.
Now the hungry lion roars,

356–357. Bergomask dance: country dance named for Bergamo, Italy.
366.   told: counted.
370.   palpable-gross: obviously grotesque.

And the wolf behowls the moon;   375
Whilst the heavy plowman snores,
    All with weary task fordone.°
Now the wasted brands do glow,
    Whilst the screech owl, screeching loud,
Puts the wretch that lies in woe   380
    In remembrance of a shroud.
Now it is the time of night,
    That the graves, all gaping wide,
Every one lets forth his sprite,
    In the churchway paths to glide: 385
And we fairies, that do run
    By the triple Hecate's team,°
From the presence of the sun,
    Following darkness like a dream,
Now are frolic. Not a mouse   390
Shall disturb this hallowed house:
I am sent, with broom, before,
To sweep the dust behind the door.°

Enter OBERON *and* TITANIA *with their train.*

Oberon.
Through the house give glimmering light,
    By the dead and drowsy fire: 395
Every elf and fairy sprite
    Hop as light as bird from brier;
And this ditty, after me,
Sing, and dance it trippingly.
Titania.
First, rehearse your song by rote,   400
To each word a warbling note:

---

377. **fordone:** worn out.
387. **triple Hecate's team:** The goddess Hecate had three names; a
     team of black horses (or dragons) pulled her chariot.
393. **behind the door:** from behind (Puck was traditionally connected
     with housecleaning and was sometimes depicted with a broom
     and a candle).

Hand in hand, with fairy grace,
Will we sing, and bless this place.

Song and dance.

Oberon.

Now, until the break of day,
Through this house each fairy stray.   405
To the best bride-bed will we,
Which by us shall blessèd be;
And the issue there create
Ever shall be fortunate.
So shall all the couples three   410
Ever true in loving be;
And the blots of nature's hand
Shall not in their issue stand.
Never mole, harelip, nor scar,
Nor mark prodigious,° such as are   415
Despisèd in nativity,
Shall upon their children be.
With this field-dew consecrate,
Every fairy take his gait,°
And each several° chamber bless,   420
Through this palace, with sweet peace,
And the owner of it blest
Ever shall in safety rest.
Trip away; make no stay;
Meet me all by break of day.   425

Exeunt OBERON, TITANIA, *and train.*

Puck.

If we shadows have offended,
Think but this, and all is mended:
That you have but slumb'red here,
While these visions did appear.

---

415. mark prodigious: ominous birthmark.
419. take his gait: go his way.
420. several: separate, individual.

And this weak and idle° theme,   430
No more yielding but° a dream,
Gentles, do not reprehend:
If you pardon, we will mend.
And, as I am an honest Puck,
If we have unearnèd luck   435
Now to scape the serpent's tongue,°
We will make amends ere long;
Else the Puck a liar call:
So, good night unto you all.
Give me your hands,° if we be friends,   440
And Robin shall restore amends.°

Exit.

---

430. **idle:** foolish.
431. **No ... but:** yielding no more than.
436. **to ... tongue:** to escape hisses from the audience.
440. **Give ... hands:** applaud.
441. **restore amends:** give satisfaction in return.

CONNECTIONS

from The Knight's Tale
from The Canterbury Tales
Geoffrey Chaucer

Stories of old have made it known to us
That there was once a Duke called Theseus,
Ruler of Athens, Lord and Governor,
And in his time so great a conqueror
There was none mightier beneath the sun.
And many a rich country he had won,
What with his wisdom and his troops of horse.
He had subdued the Amazons by force
And all their realm, once known as Scythia,
But then called Femeny. Hippolyta,
Their queen, he took to wife, and, says the story,
He brought her home in solemn pomp and glory,
Also her younger sister, Emily.
And thus victorious and with minstrelsy
I leave this noble Duke for Athens bound
With all his host of men-at-arms around.

      And were it not too long to tell again
I would have fully pictured the campaign
In which his men-at-arms and he had won
Those territories from the Amazon
And the great battle that was given then
Between those women and the Athenian men,
Or told you how Hippolyta had been
Besieged and taken, fair courageous queen,

And what a feast there was when they were married,
And after of the tempest that had harried
Their home-coming. I pass these over now
Having, God knows, a larger field to plough.
Weak are my oxen for such mighty stuff;
What I have yet to tell is long enough.
I won't delay the others of our rout,
Let every fellow tell his tale about
And see who wins the supper at the Inn.
Where I left off, let me again begin.

Queen Mab
William Shakespeare

Oh, then, I see Queen Mab hath been with you.
She is the fairies' midwife, and she comes
In shape no bigger than an agate stone
On the forefinger of an alderman,
Drawn with a team of little atomies
Athwart men's noses as they lie asleep;

Her wagon spokes made of long spinners' legs,
The cover of the wings of grasshoppers,
The traces of the smallest spider's web,
The collars of the moonshine's watery beams,
Her whip of cricket's bone, the lash of film,
Her wagoner a small, grey-coated gnat,
Not half so big as a round little worm
Prick'd from the lazy finger of a maid;
Her chariot is an empty hazelnut
Made by the joiner squirrel or old grub,
Time out o' mind the fairies' coachmakers.

And in this state she gallops night by night
Through lovers' brains, and then they dream of love;
O'er courtiers' knees, that dream in court'sies straight;
O'er lawyers' fingers, who straight dream in fees;
O'er ladies' lips, who straight on kisses dream,
Which oft the angry Mab with blisters plagues,

Because their breaths with sweetmeats tainted are.
Sometimes she gallops o'er a courtier's nose,
And then he dreams of smelling out a suit;
And sometimes comes she with a tithe pig's tail
Tickling a parson's nose as he lies asleep,
Then dreams he of another benefice.

Sometimes she driveth o'er a soldier's neck,
And then dreams he of cutting foreign throats,
Of breaches, ambuscades, Spanish blades,
Of healths five fathoms deep; and then anon
Drums in his ear, at which he starts and wakes,
And being thus frighted swears a prayer or two
And sleeps again. This is that very Mab
That plaits the manes of horses in the night
And bakes the elf locks in foul sluttish hairs,
Which once untangled much misfortune bodes,
This is she.

■ ■ ■

Midsummer Night Is More Than a Dream

Jay Walljasper

As a youngster, I was deeply intrigued by the idea of solstice—so much so that one year I made a vow to fully experience all the daylight hours of both the shortest and the longest days.

Observing winter solstice was a cinch—it was still dark at my usual rising time and the sun went to bed in the evening long before I did. The summer solstice posed more of a problem. Sunrise was so early that to see it I would need to borrow my dad's alarm clock. But that would require divulging my reasons for getting up so early and I was sure that everyone would think me really weird. I figured I was the only person in the world who cared about these non-holidays. My solution: sleep out on the picnic table (which I thought somehow seemed less odd than setting an alarm clock for 4:30 A.M.) to let the first rays of the sun wake me. It worked. I had a stiff back all day, but I did soak in each minute of sunlight on June 21.

It wasn't until many years later that I discovered that the solstices have been regarded by many cultures through history as the most important days of the year. Indeed, many of our Christmas, Chanukah, and New Year's customs are drawn from ancient solstice rituals. Even the Fourth of July, with fireworks lighting the night sky, echoes the traditional fire festivals of the summer solstice.

In many parts of the world, from Indian villages in Peru to Islamic communities in North Africa, people

commemorate the sun's peak of power with a blazing
bonfire, according to Richard Heinberg, author of
**Celebrate the Solstice: Honoring the Earth's Seasonal
Rhythms through Festival and Ceremony**. . . . The
Plains Indians of North America observed the event with
a ceremonial sun dance on the full moon closest to the
solstice; even today in New Mexico's Taos Pueblo, run-
ners clamber up a mountainside on June 21 to greet the
rising sun.

Donna Hennes, writing in **Free Spirit** magazine . . .
notes: "The Aztecs of Mexico, the Mesoamerican Maya,
the Incas of Peru, the Chinese and the Egyptians all left
architectural testimony" to their solstice observances in
the form of temples that are in perfect alignment with the
sun's path on June 21.

As with Christmas, the Christian church appropriated
this pagan celebration as a religious holiday, St. John the
Baptist Day, June 24. Yet many of the traditions of the
earlier sun festival endured, especially among rural
peasants, whose lives were intimately connected to the
rhythms of the earth. J. C. Cooper in **The Aquarian
Dictionary of Festivals** . . . notes that St. John the Baptist
celebrations involved not just bonfires but also torchlight
processions and circle dances in which people and live-
stock would leap over the bonfire flames to ensure good
luck in the coming year. For further good luck, people
donned garlands of wildflowers—especially yellow ones,
to symbolize the sun's power. Many people stayed up all
night to watch the sunrise. It was also the time when magic
herbs were traditionally gathered for use in healing.

In Britain, some midsummer traditions still survive as
part of May Day celebrations. And in Scandinavia, where
dramatic fluctuations in the amount of sunlight are such a

major factor in people's lives, midsummer rituals never died out at all. They still involve a maypole (a holdover from the days when summer solstice was a fertility festival) and, in some communities, the selection of a midsummer bride and groom. Donna Hennes notes that summer solstice was historically a lover's holiday, since children conceived then were born the following spring and had a greater chance for survival.

In Cornwall, a stronghold of Celtic traditions in southwestern England, the midsummer rites have been revived, with the hilltops blazing with bonfires. In **A Calendar of Festivals** . . . Marian Green reports that in many Cornish communities, an Earth Lady or Harvest Mother, attended by a flower-bedecked court of followers, casts a bouquet of flowers, herbs, plants, and weeds into the bonfire as a blessing for the year's crops.

There's a renewed interest in summer solstice traditions in many places, as more and more people come to realize that industrial society's distance from the processes and rhythms of nature is the root cause of our ecological crisis. . . .

Richard Heinberg thinks midsummer is the perfect time to celebrate the earth's feminine spirit because its bountiful creativity—flowers, lush foliage, maturing crops, and frisky young animals—is on full display. It might be an occasion for meditations on the goddess or a reading from the writings of some inspiring woman of the past. He suggests lighting a bonfire, or at least a few candles, to pay tribute to the sun's power—and then a hearty round of singing, dancing, and feasting. "Spend as much of your day as possible outdoors," he writes, "and make the earth, the trees, the animals, and the herbs your co-celebrants."

Donna Hennes suggests that we adapt another June
tradition to a new use. "I have a proposal to make," she
writes. "And I'm down on one knee to do it. This solstice
shall we engage in holy wedlock with the world? . . .
To love and honor and protect our most beauteous and
beloved planet? Shall we take her as our cherished bride
and stride off into a secure future of fond and careful
husbandry?"

from *Utne Reader*
July/August 1993

■ ■ ■

Woman's Constancy
John Donne

Now thou hast loved me one whole day,

Tomorrow when thou leav'st, what wilt thou say?

Wilt thou then antedate some new-made vow?

   Or say that now

We are not just those persons which we were?

Or, that oaths made in reverential fear

Of love, and his wrath, any may forswear?

Or, as true deaths true marriages untie,

So lovers' contracts, images of those,

Bind but till sleep, death's image, them unloose?

   Or, your own end to justify,

For having purposed change, and falsehood, you

Can have no way but falsehood to be true?

Vain lunatic,[1] against these 'scapes I could

   Dispute, and conquer, if I would,

   Which I abstain to do,

For by tomorrow, I may think so too.

---

1. **lunatic:** The word has for Donne the additional meaning of *inconstant* or
fickle, since lunacy (from *luna*, moon) was supposed to be affected by the
changing phases of the moon.

Tin Tan Tan

Sandra Cisneros

Me abandonaste, mujer, porque soy muy pobre
Y por tener la desgracia de ser casado.
Que voy hacer si yo soy el abandonado,
Abandonado sea por el amor de Dios.

—"El Abandonado"

Little thorn in my soul, pebble in my shoe, jewel of my life, the passionate doll who has torn my heart in two, tell me, cruel beauty that I adore, why you torment me. I have the misfortune of being both poor and without your affection. When the hope of your caresses flowered in my soul, happiness blossomed in my tomorrows. But now that you have yanked my golden dreams from me, I shiver from this chalice of pain like a tender white flower tossed in rain. Return my life to me, and end this absurd pain. If not, Rogelio Velasco will have loved in vain.

Until death do us part, said your eyes, but not your heart. All, all illusion. A caprice of your flirtatious woman's soul. I confess I am lost between anguish and forgetting. And now if I dissolve my tears in dissipation, know, my queen, only you are to blame. My fragile heart will never be the same.

Providence knew what was in store, the day I arrived innocently at your door. Dressed in my uniform and carrying the tools of my trade, without knowing destiny waited for me, I knocked. You opened your arms, my heaven, but kept your precious heart locked.

If God wills it, perhaps these words of sentiment will convince you. Perhaps I can exterminate the pests of doubt that infest your house. Perhaps the pure love I had to offer wasn't enough and another now is savoring your honeyed nectar. But none will love you so honorably and true as the way Rogelio Velasco loved you.

They say of the poet and madman we all have a little. Even my life I would give for your exquisite treasures. But poor me. Though others may lure you with jewels and riches, all I can offer is this humble measure.

Alone, all alone in the world, sad and small like a nightingale serenading the infinite. How could a love so tender and sweet become the cross of my pain? No, no, I can't conceive I won't receive your precious lips again. My eyes are tired of weeping, my heart of beating. If perhaps some crystal moment before dawn or twilight you remember me, bring only a bouquet of tears to lay upon my thirsty grave.

Tan TÁN

■ ■ ■

from The Daily Round
from How Shakespeare Spent the Day
Ivor Brown

To be in the thick of it as a player, playwright, and share-
holder was a gruelling life. There is good reason for sup-
posing that the actors in Shakespeare's time had to be
early at work. Nowadays professional actors generally
rehearse in the morning and afternoon with a short break
for a light lunch. But in Shakespeare's day the performances in the open theatres were given in the afternoon.
Thus the time for preparing the next production was awk-
wardly curtailed or broken up. The prevailing system was
a repertory with plays coming in and dropping out rapidly
according to their degree of popularity. Even those most
liked did not have 'a run,' as we call it. They were, of
course, given more often, but ten or twenty scattered performances would be taken as evidence of a considerable
hit. The more the failures, the more replacements were
needed. So there can have been few days in which rehearsals of some kind were not going on, not only in the
preparation of new plays but also in the brushing-up of
productions brought out of stock.

It has been estimated that Shakespeare's own company
staged fifteen or more new plays in a year, provided that
the year's work was not interrupted by an outbreak of
plague, the closing of the London theatres, or a departure
on a tour round the country towns. (In a way these epi-
demics may have come as a relief, since old plays could
be used afresh and there would be less rehearsal needed
and less drudgery in the learning of new parts.) Assum-
ing the estimate of fifteen new productions a year to be

correct, Shakespeare and his fellow-players, if they stayed in London and worked continuously, had just over three weeks in which to launch each new venture.

To a company engaged in contemporary British repertory that may seem ample time, since its members may be called on to be ready with a new production every fortnight and in many cases every week. But these companies are usually handling plays that have been presented previously in London and are available in print together with the stage-directions made by the original director. In that case the director of the repertory company has had a good deal of his work done for him in advance. The repertories do offer new pieces from time to time, but their novelty is not likely to be a *King Lear* or to involve fencing-matches or scenes of battle with scurrying armies. That was the kind of task that Shakespeare's team had to tackle in the stride of their tragical-historical-comical repertory. Furthermore the leading players in that company, in addition to learning and rehearsing new and long parts, were administrators and no doubt were glad to be their own masters even though it meant more worry. Their day's work included commissioning new plays, considering plays submitted, front-of-the-house management, coping with the balance of costs and takings, discovering talent, and training 'the young entry'. That again was a matter of great importance. There were, as far as we know, no academies of dramatic art, pouring out apprentices with a two years' course of instruction behind them. The companies were their own drama schools in which the boys learned as they went and by watching rehearsal and performance; but there must have been some teaching too and portions of valuable time must have been allotted to that. . . .

How, amid this hurly-burly, were the various jobs fitted into the divisions of the day? The usual daily performance was at two in the afternoon or a little later. By that time there was a sufficiency of leisured and wealthy or of poorer men with a free afternoon to create an audience. One of the epigrams of Sir John Davies, a poet and play-fancier of the period, gives a picture of an unquenchable addict of the theatre.

> *He's like a horse, which, turning round a mill,*
> *Doth always in the self-same circle tread:*
> *First, he doth rise at ten; and at eleven*
> *He goes to Gyls, where he doth eate till one;*
> *Then sees a Play till sixe, and sups at seven; .*
> *And after supper, straight to bed is gone;*
> *And there till ten next day he doth remaine,*
> *And then he dines, and sees a Comedy*
> *And then he suppes, and goes to bed againe:*
> *Thus round he runs without variety.*

It is interesting to learn that some of the plays lasted till six: if the start was at the usual time 'the two hours' traffic of our stage' mentioned in the Prologue of *Romeo and Juliet* was not a practice always observed. The subject of the epigram was obviously a good sleeper, with or without company.

Nor were the penniless less eager than the men of means to get a place at the play. There was a complaint made in 1603 by Crosse, the author of *Vertue's Common-Wealth*, that 'pinched, needy creatures, that live of almes, with scarce clothes for their backs or food for their bellies, make hard shift that they will see a play, let wife and children begge and languish in penury'. Exaggeration perhaps, but some evidence of the appetite for more than bread and meat. . . .

The usual dinner-hour was from eleven o'clock onwards. There must have been morning rehearsals of the new play in hand, unless the actors were to be up half the night, and there was then daylight by which to work. But they had surely to break off by noon: they may not have taken a large midday meal, but they had to stop for some rest and refreshment before beginning the major business of the day. They would have to be in the tiring-room well before the trumpet sounded for a start. So we can assume that rehearsals were abandoned about noon. Actors of today do not relish matinée performances. They expect a smaller audience than they look for at night and it is a drowsy time when yawning comes easily and the quickening response of a full and alert house is unlikely. But for the Tudor actors, and audiences too, this was the time to be at their liveliest and best. Heavy feeding would be a handicap.

If all were over by half past four they may, after a drink or two, have rehearsed again, in summer-time on their own open stage or in winter by candlelight in the tiring-room or some other covered premises. Since daylight was necessary in the open theatres the six-o'clock ending mentioned by Sir John Davies was not a general occurrence. By the late afternoon, whether they had been playing for three and a half hours to the public or playing for two hours or so and then rehearsing, they would be needing a good supper: after that there would be a natural readiness to linger in a tavern, drink, gossip, and talk 'shop'. But there were the new parts to be studied, a formidable piece of homework for the night hours.

Furthermore at night, possibly following an afternoon performance for the public, they might be called to serve

a special and exalted audience at Court or at a noble-
man's house. There was, for example, a presentation of
Love's Labour's Lost at Lord Cranborne's or the Earl of
Southampton's house in January, 1605. Perhaps the
severity of the weather at that time of the year limited
their work on the open-air stage of the Globe, so that
such extra engagements, which were a compliment and
well rewarded, would be welcome; and there might be a
free and generous supper to follow. But when such additional labours were ordered much hurried work in shifting
the costumes and properties and adapting the presentation
to a different kind of stage was necessary. The players
were frequently engaged in what we call 'fit-up' productions as well as in their ordinary routine on their familiar
stage. They would be used to such improvisation because
it was inevitable when they travelled the country, but any-
body who has worked in our own time on 'fit-up' tours
knows the endurances that have to be faced. And we have
cars and motor-lorries and are not dependent on horse-
power or walking or the service of a barge which had to
be loaded and unloaded on a journey to Greenwich or
Richmond. Travelling 'on the hoof', as Nashe called it,
was a familiar exercise.

Nocturnal rehearsals were obligatory when plays
were 'preferred' for performance before Queen Elizabeth
or King James at Whitehall or wherever they desired.
There was a regular series of such commanded performances after Christmas and the arrangements were passed
on by the Lord Chamberlain to the Master of the Revels,
who was responsible for the political seemliness of all
plays. Absence of comment on matters of State was
necessary to pass this censorship, whose vigilance was
keenly directed to political and religious references.

We are apt to link the ideas of censorship and sex, but the presence of the 'broad' jest and 'blue' line was not what worried authority in Tudor and Jacobean times. The quality of entertainment and of spectacle, as well as political propriety, was a matter for the application of strict standards. Their revelling Majesties were to have the best of showmanship and there were funds for procuring it.

The Laugher

Heinrich Böll

When someone asks me what business I am in, I am seized
with embarrassment: I blush and stammer, I who am other-
wise known as a man of poise. I envy people who can say: I
am a bricklayer. I envy barbers, bookkeepers and writers the
simplicity of their avowal, for all these professions speak for
themselves and need no lengthy explanation, while I am
constrained to reply to such questions: I am a laugher. An
admission of this kind demands another, since I have to
answer the second question: 'Is that how you make your
living?' truthfully with 'Yes.' I actually do make a living at
my laughing, and a good one too, for my laughing is—
commercially speaking—much in demand. I am a good
laugher, experienced, no one else laughs as well as I do,
no one else has such command of the fine points of my
art. For a long time, in order to avoid tiresome explana-
tions, I called myself an actor, but my talents in the field
of mime and elocution are so meager that I felt this desig-
nation to be too far from the truth: I love the truth, and
the truth is: I am a laugher. I am neither a clown nor a
comedian. I do not make people gay, I portray gaiety: I
laugh like a Roman emperor, or like a sensitive schoolboy,
I am as much at home in the laughter of the seventeenth
century as in that of the nineteenth, and when occasion
demands I laugh my way through all the centuries, all
classes of society, all categories of age: it is simply a skill
which I have acquired, like the skill of being able to repair
shoes. In my breast I harbor the laughter of America, the
laughter of Africa, white, red, yellow laughter—and for
the right fee I let it peal out in accordance with the director's requirements.

I have become indispensable; I laugh on records, I laugh on tape, and television directors treat me with respect. I laugh mournfully, moderately, hysterically; I laugh like a streetcar conductor or like a helper in the grocery business; laughter in the morning, laughter in the evening, nocturnal laughter and the laughter of twilight. In short: wherever and however laughter is required—I do it.

It need hardly be pointed out that a profession of this kind is tiring, especially as I have also—this is my specialty— mastered the art of infectious laughter; this has also made me indispensable to third- and fourth-rate comedians, who are scared—and with good reason—that their audiences will miss their punch lines, so I spend most evenings in night clubs as a kind of discreet claque, my job being to laugh infectiously during the weaker parts of the program. It has to be carefully timed: my hearty, boisterous laughter must not come too soon, but neither must it come too late, it must come just at the right spot: at the pre-arranged moment I burst out laughing, the whole audience roars with me, and the joke is saved.

But as for me, I drag myself exhausted to the check-room, put on my overcoat, happy that I can go off duty at last. At home I usually find telegrams waiting for me: 'Urgently require your laughter. Recording Tuesday,' and a few hours later I am sitting in an overheated express train bemoaning my fate.

I need scarcely say that when I am off duty or on vacation I have little inclination to laugh: the cowhand is glad when he can forget the cow, the bricklayer when he can forget the mortar, and carpenters usually have doors at home which don't work or drawers which are hard to open. Confectioners like sour pickles, butchers like marzipan, and the baker prefers sausage to bread; bullfighters raise pigeons for a hobby, boxers turn pale when their children have nosebleeds: I find all this quite natural, for I never laugh off duty. I am a very solemn person, and people consider me— perhaps rightly so—a pessimist.

During the first years of our married life, my wife would often say to me: 'Do laugh!' but since then she has come to realize that I cannot grant her this wish. I am happy when I am free to relax my tense face muscles, my frayed spirit, in profound solemnity. Indeed, even other people's laughter gets on my nerves, since it reminds me too much of my profession. So our marriage is a quiet, peaceful one, because my wife has also forgotten how to laugh: now and again I catch her smiling, and I smile too. We converse in low tones, for I detest the noise of the night clubs, the noise that sometimes fills the recording studios. People who do not know me think I am taciturn. Perhaps I am, because I have to open my mouth so often to laugh.

I go through life with an impassive expression, from time to time permitting myself a gentle smile, and I often won- der whether I have ever laughed. I think not. My brothers and sisters have always known me for a serious boy.

So I laugh in many different ways, but my own laughter I have never heard.

—translated by Leila Vennewitz

■   ■   ■

Mr. Moon
A Song of the Little People
Bliss Carman

O Moon, Mr. Moon,
When you comin' down?
Down on the hilltop,
Down in the glen,
Out in the clearin',
To play with little men?
Moon, Mr. Moon,
When you comin' down?
.   .   .   .

O Mr. Moon,
Hurry up along!
The reeds in the current
Are whisperin' slow;
The river's a-wimplin'
To and fro.
Hurry up along,
Or you'll miss the song!
Moon, Mr. Moon,
When you comin' down?
.   .   .   .

O Moon, Mr. Moon,
When you comin' down?
Down where the Good Folk
Dance in a ring,
Down where the Little Folk
Sing?
Moon, Mr. Moon,
When you comin' down?

■   ■   ■

The Fairies

William Allingham

Up the airy mountain,
　　Down the rushy glen,
We daren't go a-hunting
　　For fear of little men;
Wee folk, good folk,
　　Trooping all together;
Green jacket, red cap,
　　And white owl's feather!

Down along the rocky shore
　　Some make their home,
They live on crispy pancakes
　　Of yellow tide-foam;
Some in the reeds
　　Of the black mountain-lake,
With frogs for their watch-dogs,
　　All night awake.

High on the hill-top
　　The old King sits;
He is now so old and gray
　　He's nigh lost his wits.
With a bridge of white mist
　　Columbkill he crosses

On his stately journeys
From Slieveleague to Rosses;
Or going up with music
On cold, starry nights,
To sup with the Queen
Of the gay Northern Lights.

They stole little Bridget
For seven years long;
When she came down again
Her friends were all gone.
They took her lightly back,
Between the night and morrow;
They thought that she was fast asleep,
But she was dead with sorrow.
They have kept her ever since
Deep within the lake,
On a bed of flag-leaves,
Watching till she wake.

By the craggy hill-side,
Through the mosses bare,
They have planted thorn-trees
For pleasure here and there.
Is any man so daring
As dig them up in spite,
He shall find their sharpest thorns
In his bed at night.

Up the airy mountain,
    Down the rushy glen,
We daren't go a-hunting
    For fear of little men;
Wee folk, good folk,
    Trooping all together;
Green jacket, red cap,
    And white owl's feather!

■ ■ ■

from The Rebirth of Shakespeare's Globe

Richard Covington

Under a cloudless, inky sky in London, Valentine, friend of Proteus, the distinctly ungentlemanly gentleman in William Shakespeare's comedy *The Two Gentlemen of Verona*, was begging Julia to forgive Proteus for his infidelities. The sold-out audience of 1,500 inside the new Globe theater heaved a collective sigh of disgust. The couple expected to kiss and make up amid audience laughter, but the spectators had other ideas.

Suddenly, a voice from the standing crowd blurted out: "Don't do it, Julia." The actors stopped dead. In the intimacy of the open-air theater, this impassioned cry from the audience was like having an unexpected player thrust on stage—one incensed enough to rewrite the ending.

"Instead of comic relief, I felt a shiver run up my back, like I was in the presence of a lynch mob," explained Mark Rylance, the Proteus character and the Globe's 37-year-old artistic director. "When Julia said she'd take Proteus back, in determined opposition to audience wishes, there was no laughter at all. Their reaction was the absolute opposite of what we expected."

Shakespeare and the late Sam Wanamaker, coproducers of the show, must have been smiling in the wings. Once more, a Globe audience had tossed a wrench in the theatrical works.

After an absence of nearly 400 years, Shakespeare's Globe theater rises again on the South Bank of the Thames River, 200 yards from its original 1599 site. Awakening this Sleeping Beauty, the jewel in the crown of Elizabethan theater, took 27 years, only a few years less than the Wars of the Roses. The marathon campaign to resurrect the "Wooden O"—as Shakespeare's called it in *Henry V*—has been an epic adventure of dreams and disasters, fundraising nightmares, lawsuits and nitpicky scholarly debate. The efforts of the star of the drama, Sam Wanamaker, an actor, producer, and director of stage and screen, were variously branded by the project's numerous critics as crackpot, elitist, fast-buck or, more simply, flat-out impossible.

Following a "prologue" run in 1996, the Globe's first season opened last June with a nostalgic production of *Henry V* directed by a young man named Olivier. Laurence Olivier won international recognition directing himself in the 1945 film of *Henry V;* this time, his 36-year-old son, Richard, directed Rylance as the warrior king in the first play of the four-play season that ran through September.

Authentically re-created from extensive scholarly and archaeological evidence, the Globe is once again the Bard's theater. Using Elizabethan building techniques, the theater was constructed as a 20-sided polygon, 100 feet in diameter and 45 feet high, with whitewashed, half-timber walls and a thatched roof crown. Inside, three tiers of wooden benches surround an open yard and platform thrust stage.

Within the roofless theater, plays are staged in much the same way as when Shakespeare's troupe produced them—without sets, decor, microphones or spotlights, or any of the techno-wizardry and theatrical prestidigitation now standard in even the most low-budget West End musical. The sole concession is a bank of floodlights to replicate daylight for evening productions.

Performing in the new Globe has been a revelation to the actors. "It was like going to the moon, taking off your helmet and suddenly realizing there was no air," joked Lennie James, who played Valentine in last year's production

of *Two Gentlemen.* "When the audience came in, all our
rehearsal preparation seemed irrelevant. I have never performed in any play where the audience became so vocally
and physically involved."

"The audience more or less took over the production,"
added Andrew Gurr, one of the Globe's consulting scholars
and a professor at the University of Reading. "And the actors
ignore them at their peril." In this theater, actors need the
honed reflexes of a stand-up comedian; the ability to catch
audience banter from out of left field and instantly incorporate it into the action. . . .

Wanamaker first came up with the idea of rebuilding
the Globe in 1949, when he was in London to shoot a film.
Like legions of aspiring actors before him, Wanamaker's
earliest recollection of a play was Shakespeare—*King Lear*
in Yiddish, no less. He felt indebted to the playwright
who played a role in launching his career in theater and
film. He had long been curious about the location of the
original site of the Globe, and after a search in a dangerous, decrepit section of London, Wanamaker found himself peering at a sooty plaque on a brewery wall. He was
appalled. The upstart Yank tried to drum up interest in
rebuilding the Globe, but after two decades of failing to
arouse any interest, Wanamaker decided to spearhead the
thing himself.

In 1970, Wanamaker started the Globe Playhouse Trust
to raise funds. He invested his own money and promised
himself that at the first obstacle he encountered he would
drop the project. Fortunately for the Globe, he ignored his
own advice.

In 1972, he purchased an old coffee-grinding factory
near the original Globe site and set up the vest-pocket Bear
Gardens Museum (named for the bearbaiting pit that once
stood there) as a showcase promoting the nascent Globe.

Since the original Globe site was already occupied by a
functioning brewery and a historically protected Georgian-
era building, Wanamaker had to cast about for another
location for the proposed theater. After years of acrimonious
negotiations with various property developers and a lawsuit
with the local council, he emerged with a 1.2-acre site on
a street-maintenance storage yard not very far from the
site of the original Globe. Construction started on the new
Globe in 1989.

Since no detailed plans of the original Globe survived,
architects and scholars worked in a void—in spite of the
vast reams of speculation churned out about the shape of
the theater. Fortunately, meticulous perspective drawings of
the neighborhood in the early 1600s give a close approxi-
mation of the theater's exterior. For the interior, the architects depended on sophisticated guesswork and plans from
similar theaters, classical models by the Roman architect
Vitruvius in vogue at the time, and patchy archaeological
finds from the old Globe and the nearby Rose Theatre.

Nearly every aspect of the design was up for grabs.
Should the tiring-house be inside or outside the "O"?
Outside, it was decreed by scholarly councils. Should the
stage be oriented to put audiences or actors in the shade?
Actors, because it's more important that they don't squint
into the sun, and it was the orientation of the original
theater. Should the stage be rectangular or tapered at the
front? Actors argued for tapered, claiming the rectangular
stage was awkward for performances. But Peter Street,
the original carpenter, surely used the more symmetrical
rectangle, countered the builders. Architects and academics
won the day.

Days, if not weeks, were spent deciding crucial minutiae
such as how high the stage balcony should be. Massive pillars supporting the roof would dwarf anything lower than

ten feet, argued some. But if the balcony was more than nine feet high, Romeo would have a tough time scrambling up to give Juliet a kiss, others protested. Nine feet it would be.

In a phenomenally painstaking process, the builders labored to replicate the wood-frame structure using the same carpentry techniques as the Elizabethan builders, from turning the balusters to thatching the roof by hand. Like the original Globe, the half-timber building is covered with several coats of a plaster mixture of lime, sand and animal hair.

The English oak timbers were cut green and joined together so that they will season into one another. "The joints are so tight a cigarette paper couldn't slide through them," boasted architect Greenfield.

In addition to the cost and labor that went into building the theater structure itself, a large chunk of money was poured straight into the ground, unseen and certainly unsexy for fundraising purposes. Nearly $2 million went into sinking a curtain wall nearly 1,000 feet long to block seepage from the Thames River, just 65 feet away.

The stage is five feet above ground level to permit the summoning forth of demons and ghosts from a spacious underworld. A pair of wooden pillars, painted to look like marble, supports the indigo blue heavens, studded with gilt stars and crescent moons. Behind the stage is the much-disputed balcony and colonnade elaborately carved with mythological figures. A gabled roof above the balcony holds equipment for lowering gods and spirits into the action— the deus ex machina, "god from the machine," of classical theater.

The interior sports the same kind of gaudy decorative paint job favored by decorators of the time, with the wooden figures and molding splashed with eye-jarring scarlet, egg-yolk yellow, and vermilion. "The Elizabethans were madmen for painting anything they could get a brush to," according to Greenfield.

The thatched roof is the first in London since a ban was imposed in the aftermath of the Great Fire of 1666 that leveled much of the city. To pass muster with the local fire department, the peaked water-reed thatch now sprouts a spiky row of sprinklers. Fire is no idle threat: the original Globe burned to the ground in 1613 after cannon wadding discharged during a performance of *Henry VIII* ignited the roof. A second Globe was built on the same site within a year.

The new Globe can seat about 1,500—with 500 on the ground and 1,000 on the tiered benches. In Shakespeare's day, when people were physically smaller and audiences more accustomed to jostling together, twice as many spectators could squeeze into the theater's narrow confines. . . .

Contemporary Globe audiences may smell better than their Elizabethan counterparts, but judging from performances of *Two Gentlemen,* today's audiences take to the interaction as to the manner born, playing their role of histrionic chorus to the hilt.

"Just hanging onto the narrative took an immense effort," actor Aicha Kossoko explained at a rehearsal. "If the audience wasn't saying, 'Oh come on, give her a kiss,' they were booing and hissing at the sexual innuendos."

One actor needed to fill in as designated dramatic driver, holding tight to the narrative thread. "If everybody responded to the audience at the same time, all was lost," observed American actress Stephanie Roth.

As intimate as the theater is, projecting from the sprawling stage required phenomenal physical exertion. "When you first come on stage, you feel as if you're screaming at the top of your voice," said Lennie James. "But you're not at all; it's just the tremendous energy you're using that makes you think you are.

"People put their kids on the stage, bought pies during the performance, or put on their raincoats as it started to drizzle. After a while, I became inured to it all," said James. . . .

"People are hungry for a place where there is some sense of an above and a below without any particular dogma. No one can say whether Shakespeare was Catholic or Protestant, Conservative or Labour, communist or capitalist. All anyone can say is the people he depicts have a heavenly aspect and an earthly aspect and each has a soul trying to balance the two. The plays become a safe place where audiences can explore this tension."

Despite such lofty revelations and tortuous decades of preparation, the resurrected Globe may still fall short. As Sir Peter Hall ruefully pointed out: "Each age kids itself that with its authentic instruments and authentic style it has got the thing itself. Then later ages laugh at it. However faithfully the Globe is done, it will inevitably be a product of the latter part of the 20th century. There is nothing wrong in that if we admit it."

But enough negatives for now. Even Wanamaker knew the Globe, his Globe, would remain a once and future work in progress. If Shakespeare's language has spoken to the world for 400 years, why not the Globe itself, symbol and witness of the old proud presumption to re-create all the world on a stage? Life's but a poor player after all, and after enough strutting and fretting to fill a thousand stages, the Wooden O has once more found its voice.

■ ■ ■

Love Potion Number Nine
Jerry Leiber and Mike Stoller

*This song, performed by the Searchers, was a hit in the
1960s.*

I took my troubles down to Madam Ruth.
You know, that Gypsy with the gold-capped tooth.
She's got a pad down at Thirty-Fourth and Vine
Sellin' little bottles of Love Potion Number Nine.

I told her that I was a flop with chicks.
I've been this way since nineteen-fifty-six.
She looked at my palm and she made a magic sign.
She said: "What you need is Love Potion Number Nine."

She bent down and turned around and gave me a wink.
She said, "I'm gonna mix it up right here in the sink."
It smelled like turpentine and looked like India ink.
I held my nose; I closed my eyes; I took a drink.

I didn't know if it was day or night.
I started kissin' ev'rything in sight.
But when I kissed the cop down at Thirty-Fourth and Vine,
He broke my little bottle of Love Potion Number Nine.

Love Potion Number Nine;
Love Potion Number Nine;
Love Potion Number Nine.

■   ■   ■

William Shakespeare
(1564–1515)

He is the most famous writer in the world, but he left us
no journals or letters— only his poems and plays. What
we know about William Shakespeare's personal life comes
mostly from church and legal documents—a baptismal
registration, a marriage license, and records of real-estate
transactions. We also have a few remarks that others
wrote about him during his lifetime.

We know that William was born the third of eight
children, around April 23, 1564, in Stratford-on-Avon,
a market town about one hundred miles northwest of
London. His father, John, was a shopkeeper and a man of
some importance in Stratford, serving at various times as
justice of the peace and high bailiff (mayor).

William attended grammar school, where he studied
Latin grammar, Latin literature, and rhetoric (the uses of language). As far as we know, he had no further formal edu-
cation. At the age of eighteen he married Anne Hathaway,
who was eight years older than he. Some time after the
birth of their second and third children (twins), Shakespeare
moved to London, apparently leaving his family in Stratford.

We know that several years later, by 1592, Shakespeare
had become an actor and a playwright. By 1594, he was
a charter member of a theatrical company called the Lord
Chamberlain's Men, which later became the King's Men.
Shakespeare worked with this company for the rest of
his writing life. Year after year he provided it with plays,
almost on demand. Shakespeare was the ultimate professional writer. He had a theater that needed plays, actors
who needed parts, and a family that needed to be fed.

Shakespeare most likely wrote *A Midsummer Night's Dream* in the mid 1590s, fairly early in his great career. Previously he had written *Richard III* and *Romeo and Juliet;* later came *The Merchant of Venice, Julius Caesar, Hamlet, Othello, King Lear,* and *Macbeth. A Midsummer Night's Dream* remains a favorite of audiences because of its touching and amusing characters and lovely language. The nineteenth-century composer Felix Mendelssohn composed popular symphonic music to accompany performances of the play.

Shakespeare died on April 23, 1616, possibly right on his fifty-second birthday. He is buried under the old stone floor in the chancel of Holy Trinity Church in Stratford. Carved on a stone over his grave is the following verse (spelling modified):

Good Friend, for Jesus' sake forbear
To dig the dust enclosed here.
Blessed be the man that spares these stones
And cursed be he that moves my bones.

These are hardly the best of Shakespeare's lines (if indeed they are his at all), but like his other lines, they seem to have worked: His bones lie undisturbed to this day. Yet Shakespeare lives on, for his plays are still frequently produced all over the world.

■ ■ ■